ADVANCE PRAISE FOR
CLASS OF '77

"The Peking University classmates of Jaime FlorCruz gave him a front-row seat in the tumultous political arena of China's post-Mao era. The Class of '77 is unique for FlorCruz's memorable first-hand accounts of knowing some of China's movers and shakers in their youth."

— Melinda Liu, Newsweek China correspondent

"Jaime FlorCruz captures the flavor and drama of his own experience in this fascinating land, the look and feel of countryside and campus, and the whole crazy, compelling sweep of China's recent history."

— Donald Morrison, former TIME International Editor

"Just after setting foot in China, Jaime FlorCruz realized his life was about to change. It was 1971 and the Cultural Revolution was roaring through the land, but Jaime embraced his new homeland and went on to serve as China bureau chief for TIME and CNN. And he was always generous with his information – Mao's wife killed herself ? Yesterday, Jaime said. Yet another FlorCruz scoop. This memoir tells us how he did it."

— Ed Gargan, former New York Times correspondent and author of *"China's Fate"*

"Only Jaime FlorCruz could write this sweeping memoir: a radical student exiled in Maoist China during the Cultural Revolution, his heart broken by not one but two Chinese lasses, eventually heads CNN's Beijing bureau."

— Jan Wong, author of *Red China Blues*

"Having served as president of the Foreign Correspondents Club of China, the Beijing bureau chief of TIME magazine and of CNN, Jimi has long been an inspiration to many young China-based foreign correspondents. He has spent more than four decades in China and understands the country inside out, and this book masterfully tells the story of how he came to grips with the dragon."

— Benjamin Lim, The Straits Times,
Global Affairs Correspondent

The Class of '77

How my classmates changed China

Jaime A. FlorCruz

EARNSHAW
BOOKS

The Class of '77

By Jaime A. FlorCruz

ISBN-13: 978-988-8769-41-4

HISTORY / Asia / China

EB147

Published by Earnshaw Books Ltd. (Hong Kong)

To my father Cenon, who encouraged me to seek education wherever the search took me.

To my mother Lourdes, who reluctantly woke me up to catch my flight to China, not knowing we wouldn't see each other again for many years.

To my wife Ana, son Joseph and daughter Michelle, who accompanied me on my remarkable China journey.

To my three granddaughters Jayden, Jazelle and Jolie, children of Janet Correa and Joseph, who inspired me to finish this book so that they may know more about their Lolo Jaime.

PROLOGUE

In 1971, I journeyed into the People's Republic of China on what was supposed to be a three-week study tour. I was a student activist in the Philippines and knew little about China. I never imagined it would be another twelve years until I was able to go home again to the Philippines or that I would spend most of my life in Communist China.

I went when Chairman Mao was in power, and the tumultuous Cultural Revolution was still in progress. Over the next fifty years, I had a ring-side seat to the most remarkable economic and social transformation in human history. I watched the rise of China under Deng Xiaoping and his successors from the ashes of the Cultural Revolution, and witnessed its transformation from one of the poorest, most isolated countries in the world to a renascent global power.

I started my journey as a student and ended as head of TIME Magazine and of CNN in China. But what really transformed my life was being part of Peking University's rightfully famous Class of '77.

This is my story — and our story. This is the story of the Class of '77.

1

THROUGH THE GATE

ON A SUNNY, nippy day in October 1977, I walked into the West Gate of Peking University with much anticipation. The palace-style portal, painted in vermillion, evokes the university's long and storied past. A big plaque hangs in the middle of the gate with the name of the university carved in four Chinese characters, "Bei Jing Da Xue"—Peking University—in the calligraphy of Chairman Mao. I was there to enroll as a freshman in the Class of 1977.

I proceeded to look for the Foreign Students Office, my first stop to register. I crossed a small stone bridge over a moat dotted by lotus plants. Cicadas were chirping, frogs croaking. Yellow leaves blown off by the brisk autumn wind covered the sidewalks of the narrow road. A stone statue of Chairman Mao towered in front of quaint old buildings painted in red and white and topped with pagoda-style roofs. Further down, behind the traditional-style buildings, was the charming Weiming Lake.

Days earlier, I made a special trip to the Youyi (Friendship) Photo Studio, near Tiananmen Square, to get ID photos taken, then proceeded to the Capital Hospital for a medical checkup. I also made photocopies of my diploma and transcripts from the Beijing Languages Institute, where I had recently completed a three-year course in Chinese language and translation. Peking

University required all of them for enrollment.

Cai Huosheng, a stocky fifty-something staff officer of the Foreign Students Office, greeted me at the door.

"You're the only student we are enrolling from the Philippines this year," he said, as I handed him the required documents. "Welcome. Welcome."

He volunteered to show me around for orientation. We walk past the Library and a classroom building, where scores of students are on a break. Most wore blue and green Mao jackets and baggy pants. They were lined up on the sidewalk doing calisthenics in synch with the staccato music blaring from the university's PA system. It was the same prescribed group exercise that we used to do in the Beijing Languages Institute. I noted that the students were mostly older, looking to be in their late twenties and early thirties. Some wore PLA military uniforms.

"They are the *gong-nong-bing* students," Teacher Cai explained, referring to the Worker-Peasant-Soldier college students on campus. "They may be the last batch of that cohort."

When the Cultural Revolution started in 1966, all universities were closed, and the *gaokao*, the national college entrance exam started in 1952, was abruptly scuttled. Some schools, like Peking University, reopened in 1970, but only to enrollees recommended by their work units—the people's communes, factories and the military—based on their work attitude and political correctness. Based on this recommendation system, those who had "bad" family background need not apply. Tests, deemed elitist, were taboo.

By the summer of 1977, about a year after Mao's death, the news came that the *gaokao* examination for college entry would resume. Because there was little time to prepare for the first nationwide college entrance exam since 1965, the planned tests were moved back to November and December 1977. That meant my Class of 1977 cohorts would not be able to enroll until Spring 1978, after they had passed the *gaokao*.

"Meantime, you may get started by taking up core subjects with the Worker-Peasant-Soldier class," Cai advised.

The next day, I was back in Peking University, carrying my hardcase luggage containing all my possessions. This time, I walked into the South Gate, close to Building 26, the three-story dormitory building reserved for male foreign students. The grey-colored brick structure would be my home for the next four years.

Teacher Cai met me there and led me to Room 346. I was assigned to stay in this ten-square-meter room furnished with two wooden beds, a closet as well as a pair of worktables and chairs. I was also given a wash basin, a towel, and a thermos bottle.

"The communal washroom and toilet are right next door," Teacher Cai said. I felt like an army recruit receiving the standard issues. "You will share this room with a Chinese student who is also enrolled in the history department. He can help you with class work."

Meantime, I awaited the arrival of my Class of 1977 cohorts with keen anticipation.

Cai handed me my student pin and ID card. The red plastic cover was embossed in gold with the four characters in Mao's calligraphy for Peking University. It identified me as "Ji Mi" (literally, Lucky Rice), a student from the Philippines in the history department. It was issued on October 8, 1977 by the Peking University Revolutionary Committee.

I felt a sense of triumph. For years, I had wanted to get into Peking University. Founded in 1898 as the first national university in China's modern history, it is also known as the "Harvard of China". It enjoys an excellent reputation as an institution of higher education and research. Finally, it was happening, and I would be a part of The Class of 1977.

Deng Xiaoping, purged by Mao Zedong during the Cultural Revolution and rehabilitated as Vice Premier in 1977, had pushed to restore the college entrance exam. Many in the leadership supported the idea, but others had qualms.

China in 1977 was in a state of flux. On September 9, 1976, Chairman Mao passed away at age 84. Weeks later, the radical faction of the Gang of Four, led by his widow Jiang Qing, were arrested by Deng Xiaoping's loyalists in the Communist Party and the military. Deng, whom Mao had vilified and purged from top posts, made a political comeback, promising massive changes. What was in store after Mao? No one knew for sure.

There was elation mixed with jitters. Days after the news of the Gang of Four's downfall spread in the Chinese capital, many of my Chinese friends gathered with family and friends to share celebratory meals. Some set off fireworks, others opened bottles of *Er Guo Tou*, a cheap liquor made of sorghum, to cheer the end of the Maoist era.

There were early signs that things were starting to look up. There was a significant increase in the variety of food available, although truckloads of cabbage—staples for Beijing residents through winter—were still to be seen everywhere. In a few places in central Beijing, propaganda billboards and signages, mostly hortatory quotations from Mao, the Great Helmsman, had been quietly pulled down or replaced. Still, a huge concrete billboard, painted in bold Chinese characters, stood at the corner of the National Art Museum: "Educated youth must go down the countryside to get reeducation from the poor and lower middle peasants."

Year 1977 was a cathartic year of change. Once a stagnant country, China in that year began to percolate with pent-up

4

energy and unfulfilled ambitions. The 1977 *gaokao* was hugely symbolic of that historic turnaround. That generation of exam-takers, hungry for knowledge and seeking a better life, would soon ignite decades of growth, turmoil and reform. Most entrants were young people whose schooling had been disrupted by the Cultural Revolution. Many had endured hardships in factories or in the countryside. Some were languishing in boring clerical jobs in the bureaucracy. That year, 5.7 million people sat through days of competitive exams. Only 4.8 per cent of them passed. That was the first generation of college students in twelve years who were admitted based on academic merit. It was the first time that they were given the chance — for some, the last chance — to change their destiny. Most were already in their twenties, or even thirties. Some already had children. Years later, thanks to their grit, intellect and resilience, many of this generation joined the elite in politics, education, military, business, art and culture. They took up the responsibility to help China avoid dystopia and instead enter a period of rejuvenation.

They became known as the Class of '77.

In the four years I spent studying at Peking University, I met many outstanding members of this cohort. They eventually became shock-troops of Deng Xiaoping's reform and pioneers of China's modernization drive and would form the backbone of China's professional contingent in different walks of life. Some would work within the system; others would work to overturn the system. If I had been in the wrong place at the wrong time on August 21, 1971, this time I was in the right place at the right time, seated in the front-row witnessing a superpower's awakening and rise.

Our schoolmates at Peking University followed many different trajectories. My classmate Bo Xilai, like me a history major, would become a political superstar touting a Maoist revival, if only in spirit, having led one large city and a huge province to economic development success. Wang Juntao, an *enfant terrible* of the Physics department, was twenty-two years old at the start of classes, one of the youngest enrollees and a whiz at nuclear science. But his passion proved to be politics, and he evolved quickly into an evangelist of democracy. Also in Bo's and Wang's batch at the university was Li Keqiang, later to become China's premier, the second-most powerful person in the country, at least in name. Bo would soar incredibly high and then suffer a scandalous collapse. Li remained in power by maintaining, for the most part, a colorless public persona as he imposed technocratic discipline on the country. And Wang ended up in jail, and then exile in the United States. Each was an example of what Wang declared was our school's spirit: "Conquer or die."

More than school spirit, there was an energizing force behind the particular class that Wang, Bo, Li and I belonged – the Peking University Class of 1977. The stories of Wang, and Bo, and Li are bound up in the saga of the university and of the fate of China itself and beyond. This shared mission – to take part in China's renewed quest to modernize – is key to understanding Li Keqiang and his path to power. It explains the impetus behind Bo Xilai's spectacular rise and fall. It is why Wang Juntao lives in exile in the United States. It is how a man with the surname FlorCruz ended up as one of the most visible foreign journalists operating in China.

But to understand the Class of '77, one also has to know what came to an end the year before. In 1976, China was still staggering from the cataclysm of the Great Proletarian Cultural Revolution, which Mao Zedong unleashed in August 1966. On one level, it was Mao's attempt to convert people's "feudal" or "bourgeois" thinking into a new, proletarian mindset. But its real purpose was to purge from the Communist Party leadership all the so-called "capitalist roaders" and "revisionists" — that is, those who opposed Mao's authority and policies. Millions of teenage Red Guards ravaged the country, following Mao's admonition to "bombard the headquarters" and "root out class enemies." They targeted party officials, government bureaucrats and intellectuals. They inflicted detention, torture and death on millions of innocents. Meanwhile, Mao's radical ideologues instructed ordinary Chinese to study a pocket-size red book, the Quotations from Chairman Mao, which they memorized and recited like an all-purpose mantra. Defense minister Lin Biao, Mao's designated successor, compared the Little Red Book, to a "spiritual atom-bomb."

The tumultuous campaign ripped apart the fabric of Chinese society and tradition. A country that honored elders for their instruction and the past for its wisdom was torn asunder by the Red Guards, the youthful bands of marauders empowered to inflict the latest ideological innovation concocted by Mao, founder of the People's Republic who ruled the realm like an infallible god-king. At its hysterical peak, the Cultural Revolution turned into a nationwide witch-hunt of "class enemies". Children turned on parents; friend on friend; neighbor on neighbor – all in the name of Maoist rectitude, all to prove that the accuser was Redder than Thou.

The result was close to self-destruction. As radical Red Guards rampaged across the country, schools, universities and research centers closed down. Farmers and workers were swamped with incessant political and ideological campaigns at the expense of production. The economy teetered on the brink of collapse. Living standards fell. Many Chinese lost their lives in factional fighting, political persecution, famine and starvation.

By the summer of 1971, China was just beginning to recover

from the chaos that the Cultural Revolution created. Chairman Mao, desperate to pull back from anarchy, had dispatched People's Liberation Army officers to take control of local governments, factories, schools and farms. He reined in the Red Guards by sending them to farms and factories for "reeducation through labor." He allowed the radical phase of Cultural Revolution to peter out. Meanwhile, Zhou Enlai, Mao's *primus inter pares* who served as China's premier running the government, started the long, slow process of putting the house back in order. He called back some de-frocked scholars, scientists, technocrats and cadres from the reform-through-labor farms to resume work. He re-opened some schools and universities. He resumed unofficial talks with the United States and other Western countries.

The first targets of the mob had been the Chairman's political rivals, who were publicly humiliated, assaulted and, sometimes, killed or forced to commit suicide. But very quickly, every level of Chinese society was scoured for enemies of Mao Zedong's totalitarian philosophy. The universities were shut down or became showcases of mind-numbing propaganda and political sloganeering. Vast numbers of China's best and brightest were sent into internal exile in the countryside, compelled to learn from a peasantry that was extolled for its very lack of urbanity. Already poor, China had become an enormous prison for its own people, an ever more impoverished, economic dead zone, isolated from the rest of humanity, just as North Korea is today, but, with nearly a quarter of the world's population at the time, entirely more immense.

By 1976, ordinary people were longing for a final end of the Maoist madness. And the year promised—at least to the superstitious—to be portentous. It was the Chinese Lunar Year of the Fire Dragon, which comes once every six decades. The dragon, already the symbol of the country's imperial past, combined with the unpredictable element of fire to become an augury of tumult. Past years of the fire dragon had seen Chinese politics transformed. Would the same happen in 1976? In fact, the country would literally tremble.

In 1976, I was closing in on the fifth anniversary of an involuntary stay in the People's Republic, prevented by politics and bureaucracy from returning to my homeland, the Philippines. My aim, as the Chinese say, was "to turn a bad thing into a good thing," transform adversity into opportunity. I seemed to be doing well on the turnaround process. By mid-July, I had completed a three-year course in Mandarin and translation at the Beijing Languages Institute. While I waited to know what my next career move will be, the government, which closely watched the movements of all foreigners as well as citizens, moved me from the school's dormitory to the Peace Hotel on Goldfish Lane, a building that had once been the residence of a prince from the last imperial dynasty. In the labyrinth of chambers where nobles once lived, I was assigned a single room just off the main courtyard.

There was little palatial about the accommodation, however, despite the building's pedigree and its proximity to the Forbidden City, the extravagant fortress that was once the heart of the empire. The walls of the Peace Hotel were brick plastered over with a mud-and-hay mixture and a coat of grayish paint. A decade of the Cultural Revolution had ensured that almost everything was drab and utilitarian. But the hotel was, however, more comfortable than the communal facilities I had shared with other foreigners at the Language Institute's dormitory. My new lodgings had a large writing table and even space for a bathtub.

In the early morning of July 28, while it was yet dark, the Peace Hotel shook with the tremors of an enormous earthquake. My bed began to roll and the walls squeaked dangerously. I jumped out of bed and ducked under the writing table. I'd learned about what to do in a quake back in the Philippines, where I'd been through a big one before I left for China. When the rocking subsided, I rushed into the courtyard, joining other shocked and shaken guests. Hotel attendants told us to move into a van parked in the middle of an open space while we all waited for news and instructions. A senior hotel manager would only confirm that northern China had indeed been hit by a huge earthquake, with the epicenter not far away from the capital.

With aftershocks hitting again and again, all city residents took to sleeping outdoors. The weather made conditions dismal: the sky grayed and rain fell. Hotel guests were moved into military tents hurriedly pitched by the People's Liberation Army inside the grounds of the Working People's Cultural Palace, the eastern section of the Forbidden City. Chinese residents put up temporary shelters in the city's sidewalks and parks. In subsequent days, expatriates in Beijing who had access to short-wave radios slowly learned more details about the disaster.

The earthquake had leveled the city of Tangshan, a city with a population of nearly 1 million people, just 125 miles away from Beijing. Hundreds of thousands were dead, one of the worst tolls of an earthquake in history.

The cataclysm that wiped out Tangshan was only the most violent of the bad portents of 1976. There had already been one on the first week of January: Zhou Enlai, China's beloved premier, had died of cancer at age 78. To many Chinese, Zhou had been the one rational voice left in the upper echelons of the regime, the man who prevented the country from falling completely into the abyss of the Cultural Revolution. No one could actually say that out loud, of course, because the Cultural Revolution had been approved by none other than Mao, the Chairman of the all-encompassing Communist Party.

At his death, Zhou had been trying to rebuild the Communist Party's moderate and reformist faction, to make it strong enough to oppose and defeat the radicals in the party. In 1973, he had finally convinced Mao that the Cultural Revolution may have gone too far; and that, given the moribund state of the economy, it would be wise to rehabilitate Deng Xiaoping, a proponent of reform whom Mao hated and had purged from the party as the Red Guard madness inundated China.

But the radicals were not going to concede their hold on power. The avenging angels of the Cultural Revolution were embodied in a quartet of the Chairman's ideological and personal favorites, led by his wife Jiang Qing, a former actress who had become one of the most rabid instigators of Red Guard atrocities. As the communist emperor's health waned, many Chinese believed that his empress was maneuvering to assume power.

Political power had always come in just one way: through Mao's authority and approval. But by 1976, everyone knew the emperor would soon die. That inevitability did not fill them with sadness but with anxiety and fear. By contrast, the Chinese people were genuinely heartbroken by the death of Zhou, because they saw him as having been genuinely trying to save China. What would come after Mao now that Premier Zhou's steadying hand was gone?

None of my Chinese friends would speak openly of what would happen once Mao died, if only because discussing a China without the "Great Leader" was likely to attract the attention of the authorities and mark you as a menace to public order. But I could sense signs of a sagging morale among my Chinese friends. They were weary of the radical faction's relentless efforts to politicize every aspect of their lives. In public, they feigned compliance and loyalty to the leadership. In the privacy of their homes, they talked of Jiang Qing and her allies with contempt and derision.

In the days after the great earthquake, the Chinese government evacuated virtually all foreigners from Beijing, sending them to various cities in southern China on extended "tours." This was mainly to keep us from potentially hearing and seeing more from Tangshan and spreading news overseas of the government's struggle to cope with the after-effects of the disaster. Some of us stayed away from Beijing for a few weeks, others longer.

I ended up in the central province of Hunan, where Mao was born in 1893. I mostly stayed in the city of Changsha, the provincial capital, and in Hengyang, the city close to the Xiangjiang State Farm where I had worked for almost a year as a farmer after I realized I would not be able to return to the Philippines. Back then, in 1972, I had joined hundreds of Chinese youth, fresh graduates from high schools, to "receive reeducation through labor" by working with the local farmers. It was part of the "settle down in the countryside" campaign that Mao pushed to new heights during the Cultural Revolution. Hunan was steeped in ideological fervor and loyalty to Mao. Local folks seemed fairly content, even if life was poor.

I was in Hengyang on September 9, 1976, the day Chairman Mao died. I was staying in a hostel that was an hour's drive from the Xiangjiang state farm. I expected an immediate outpouring of public grief, much like the mourning I witnessed in Beijing when Zhou died nine months earlier. But in Hengyang's streets I found little signs of sadness. Some people started to put up black-and-white banners emblazoned with slogans like "Chairman Mao's spirit will live forever." I noticed some residents had put on white paper flowers and black armbands. But I did not see people sobbing or wailing.

On the day of Mao's funeral, I attended a memorial ceremony organized by the management of the Hengyang Guest House, the three-story hostel where I was lodged. The ceremony was held in synch with the main one in Beijing — just like every single memorial service in the country that day. As a boom-box played the funeral music, we all stood passively inside a meeting room hung with a huge portrait of Mao and a black-and-white banner admonishing people to "Turn grief into strength."

What happened next was astonishing. In October, the generals arrested Mao's widow, Jiang Qing, and her three ideological allies — who were then designated the "Gang of Four" as state-controlled media began a propaganda drive to discredit them, the radical faction of the party, and the Cultural Revolution itself. Eventually, the Gang of Four would stand trial and be found guilty of treason. Powerless but still haughty, Jiang Qing insisted in her televised trial — to the embarrassment of the party — that she did only as Mao instructed her to do, that the Cultural Revolution was the Chairman's scheme. "I was Chairman Mao's dog," she declared. "Whoever he told me to bite, I bit." Imprisoned and dying of cancer, she committed suicide in 1991. Our Beijing bureau's reporting team would break the news of the death of that remarkable woman to the West, one of my first scoops as a correspondent for TIME magazine in Beijing.

The reformist faction, strengthened by the fall of the Gang of Four, lobbied successfully to bring Deng Xiaoping back to Beijing in late 1976. And it was the wily Deng who managed to build up sufficient backing from the military to emerge as China's uncontested leader by the end of 1978. He would then usher in the reforms that took China from the near-death experience of the Cultural Revolution to decades of growth that have astonished the world.

Back in September 1976, none of us — my friends in Beijing or the attendees at Mao's mourning ceremony in Hengyang — could have foreseen the transformation of China from Maoist dystopia to economic superpower. I was still trying to figure out what the political developments meant for my ability to return to the Philippines. In hindsight, 1976 proved to be pivotal for me and for all the Chinese men and women of my generation. I would still be trapped in China and would not be able to travel to the Philippines for close to another decade. But actions and changes set in motion in 1976 would lead in the next year to the revival of China's moribund universities, free of the radicalism that had rendered them virtually useless as founts of learning for so many years. The freshmen who entered college that year would begin the rebuilding of the People's Republic. The members of the Class of '77 were survivors of the Cultural Revolution: they carried the lessons of that cataclysm, a perspective that colors their approach to politics, power, and the meaning of life.

2

BEIDA

JUST NORTH of what today is Beijing's Fourth Ring Road is Haidian, a bustling business and technology district studded with decorative, man-made ponds and the campuses of some of the most famous universities in China. A number of the ponds are so extensive that they are, with much poetic license, called "hai" — that is, seas. The Manchu emperors had them constructed as part of their enormous pleasure gardens. Weiming Lake isn't big enough to be called a sea. It's just a lake — or *hu* — built in the eighteenth century by a Manchu prince. Weiming is contrarian from conception: it means "without a name." Yet the shores of the lake with no name are now home to an institution that is extremely proud of its name and its reputation.

The institution is Peking University. Not Beijing University, even though "Beijing" is now the official transliteration of the city once called "Peking" by many Westerners. The spelling is a reminder of the school's origins and its historic mission: it was founded in 1898 as part of the Manchu regime's attempt — too little too late — to speed up reforms in imperial China. The empire had fallen behind Western science and learning. Its cultural and educational institutions lagged, incapable of competing with their foreign counterparts. Inspired by Japan's rapid advancement after it opened up to the West, Chinese reformers declared they wanted "Chinese learning for the essence, Western learning for the application," echoing the Japanese slogan "Eastern Ethics and Western Science." They convinced the young emperor, Guangxu, to decree a string of stirring reforms, including opening modern schools, promoting science and commerce, and sending Chinese youths to study overseas. The effort proved to be short-lived. Conservatives led by the Empress Dowager Cixi staged a coup and turned Emperor Guangxu into a virtual prisoner on an island in one of the capital's large ponds. It is one of the more poignant lessons taught to young Chinese about what one might have to suffer in the service of the country.

But the university that Guangxu brought into being during the Hundred Days of Reform has prevailed. Peking University was its name in English, and thus it has remained, as students and alumni quickly correct anyone who makes the mistake of calling it "Beijing University." (Rival and neighbor Tsinghua University, almost as old, is just as persnickety. In today's official pinyin, Tsinghua is written Qinghua). Of course, the name is the same in Chinese, regardless of how the characters are transliterated. And the first syllables of the Chinese name — *Beijing Daxue* in Mandarin pronunciation — combine to form the famous nickname the school is referred to throughout the Chinese-speaking world: Beida.

To this day, Peking University and its students have always taken pride being at the vanguard of China's quest for progress, of being first to reach for the new. The school has produced three Nobel prize winners in physics and medicine. Some of the country's most important modern writers and philosophers have worked or taught at Beida, including the iconoclastic short story writer Lu Xun, and the philosopher Hu Shih. There is a statue on campus of Li Dazhao, the head of the university's library who also founded the Chinese Communist Party in 1921. Mao Zedong worked in the university's library too, but in a minor post in the reading room. An enormous statue of Mao once stood in front of the four-story library. But in the late 1980s, about a decade after his death, the statue was quietly taken down. Another statue of the late Great Leader stands in a less prominent corner of the campus, a symbol of the way he and his legacy have been finessed in the years since.

Beida's physical appearance is constrained by a government decree banning the construction of high-rise buildings in the area around the Old Summer Palace, or Yuanmingyuan, and the Summer Palace, both nearby. The rival school, Tsinghua University, is just beyond the perimeter of the old palace grounds and its buildings can be built higher. Nevertheless, in recent decades the university campus has seen a boom in a low-rise mix of traditional and modern facilities, including Centennial Hall, and the Guanghua Business School. The Stanford Center, built with donations from Chinese alumni of the California university, is co-administered by the two universities. It manages to have three stories, with an additional two built underground. The grounds of Beida's law school have expanded as well in the past few decades. That school traces its ancestry to Peking University's law department, which was founded in 1904. As I discovered when I first went there, the teaching of law—and needless to say, of business—was sharply curtailed during the Cultural Revolution.

Beida students were prominent among the boisterous students who occupied the center of the city for two months from April 1989, but the university and its students had also been at the forefront of the Cultural Revolution twenty years earlier. "Big Character Posters"— screaming criticisms and diatribes posted in enormous blocks of text on walls, and a key feature of the era—were conceived by Nie Yuanzi, a female professor at Peking University in May 1966. Immediately after the Great Proletarian Cultural Revolution was inaugurated in August 1966, Peking University students were marching with banners and slogans, yelling out of megaphones their eternal support for Mao, and hunting for members of the enemy classes (landowners, capitalists and the bourgeoisie). Beida was always at the forefront of the quest for Chinese modernity, even when it took a wrong turn.

I first visited Beida at the end of August 1971, five years after the Cultural Revolution began. The university was one of the scheduled stops in a three-week study tour of China arranged by the China Friendship Association, a quasi-governmental Chinese agency set up to "promote friendship and understanding" with groups from foreign countries. I was one of fifteen people in what the Chinese called the "Philippine Youth Delegation," an unofficial collection of students, activists, and young professionals. At the time, relations between the Philippines and China were non-existent. Manila was an ally of the United States in the Cold War, recognized the Nationalist government of Taiwan as the legitimate ruler of the mainland, and provided Washington with two major military bases that could easily launch attacks on Communist China. The People's Republic, on the other hand, was believed to be giving, at the least, ideological support to the New People's Army, a guerrilla movement sworn to overthrow the government of Philippine President Ferdinand Marcos. All of us on the trip were acutely aware of the risks we were taking by traveling to China. The Marcos government could have us arrested upon our return to the Philippines and branded us as subversives.

In China, however, we were tourists, learning the egalitarian ways of the Communist giant. Along with Beida, we also went to Tiananmen Square, the Forbidden City, the Ming Tombs and the Great Wall. We visited the Great Hall of the People, walked through an underground air-raid shelter in the Qianmen district to the south of the Square, toured the largest steel plant in the city, visited the Capital Iron and Steel Mill, rode the underground subway line and inspected the Peking No. 2 Cotton Mill. We were fêted with many sumptuous banquets and had our fill of Peking duck.

I was impressed by the grandeur of China's past. But, as a twenty-year old student leader at a Philippine university with its fair share of political activists, I was much more interested in finding out about the Chinese revolution, and how the still-ongoing Cultural Revolution was progressing. I found the various manifestations of Maoism quite confusing. The Red Guards and the students that I met wanted to turn China into a socialist paradise, and yet they abhorred what they labeled derisively as "book learning." They spoke of "unity and friendship among the peoples of the world," but also insisted on the importance of waging "class struggle." I could sense, but had trouble understanding, the radical political, social and economic experiments underway in the country. I was particularly intrigued by the "revolution in education" that our hosts frequently cited as taking place at Peking University. At times, the conversations seemed like outtakes from an Orwell novel.

A brigade of university officials, professors and students awaited us when our tour bus pulled into the Beida campus, which had elements of both a quaint little town and a military barracks. As we got off the bus, our hosts broke out into applause and shook our hands enthusiastically. A large banner with Chinese characters was spread over the front of a large building: "Long live the friendship between the Youths of China and the Philippines." I couldn't understand a word of Chinese, though I was fascinated by the language. I didn't know then, of course, that I would be spending the next five years learning it, on farms, in school, and on a boat.

The welcoming group was led by Professor Zhou Peiyuan, the university's grey-haired chancellor, who was officially introduced as the "Vice Chairman" of the university's "Revolutionary Committee." (A Communist Party leader, not an academic, served as the Chairman.) The septuagenarian Zhou was a theoretical physicist who graduated from University of Chicago and Caltech in 1926 before returning to China, motivated by patriotism.

Speaking to us both in English and in Chinese (through an interpreter), Zhou told the story of Beida's past including its birth in 1898 as the Qing emperor Guangxu's instrument of national reform and progress. Then a couple of Chinese students spoke of the present day, saying "Beida is the base of the Red Guard movement and the political struggle against the revisionist political line of Liu Shaoqi."

I had no idea what they were talking about and only much later discovered that Liu Shaoqi was a party leader who had advocated economic reforms and had been President of China before being attacked as a "capitalist roader" by the radicals at the forefront of the Cultural Revolution. He died under mysterious circumstances in 1969, a passing that would not be known in public until years later.

But between the ideological jargon, the formulaic political phrases, and the stiltedness of the translations, I sensed the pride the students took in their struggle against "revisionism," and was mystified by it. After the welcome, Professor Zhou and the reception team took us around the campus and into classrooms, dormitories, labs and the library. We were allowed to ask about university life: How many people to a room in students' dorms? (Eight) What courses were offered? (Several, but not law, business and psychology) What does a typical day look like for students? (They started in the morning with collective jogging, and ended with lights-out early, with few nighttime activities.) As the editor of my school paper in the Philippines, I asked if Beida had its own student newspaper. No, was the answer, but students posted political propaganda, cartoons and announcements on bulletin boards set up on strategically located walls around the campus.

We were provided with many statistics and my colleagues and I took copious notes. There were 2,667 students at the university at the time (down from 10,000 when Beida was closed in 1966) and they were taught by 2,000 faculty members and staff. The university had seventeen departments, ten of which were in the social sciences and arts (Chinese literature, philosophy, history) and seven in the natural sciences (physics, chemistry, metallurgy, electronics). Law and business were not offered because, we were told, those pursuits were considered "bourgeois" or "capitalist."

The makeup of the student body was curious as well. First, all the young people who welcomed us were freshmen because Beida had been closed for the first five years of the Cultural Revolution and our visit took place in the first year classes had resumed. None of them had to take an entrance test to gain admission—a surprising development given that China was the historic originator of the concept of qualifying public service examinations. Many of the students we met had spent two to three years working in farms and factories; most of them, they said, got into Beida on the recommendation of the farmers and laborers they had worked with. Other students had previously served in the army and were similarly recommended.

The prerequisites for admission were simple: good health, work experience, and high "political consciousness." Academic prowess was much less important than a student's commitment to the ideals of the Chinese revolution and to the belief that working with one's hands was better than book learning. As part of what Beida officials called the concept of "open-door schooling," students were expected to extend their education beyond the classroom and to engage in street cleaning, farming, and assisting factory laborers with compiling "revolutionary histories" of their workplaces. These would help develop their moral, physical, ideological and intellectual character, we were told.

The guiding principle for all the subjects was a rigid Maoist perspective, including the doctrines of "combining theory with practice," of "learning by doing," and of "being socially relevant." The reception committee, for example, proudly showed us a college-run electronic equipment factory that was experimenting with, and producing, all-purpose meters and silicon-controlled rectifiers, a sort of primitive microchip. It was an example, it was stated, of the physics students combining theory with practice.

Students said that high grades were unimportant. Academic performance was rated as excellent, good, or fair but no one failed. Each class automatically moved from one level to another every year. Individual achievement was downplayed. Assignments were completed collectively, including the writing of essays and even sitting for examinations. In another break with tradition, where it once used to take four or six years to complete a degree like physics, the requirement had been reduced to two or three years, "depending on the needs of the industries."

For the members of the Philippine Youth Delegation, one noteworthy element of Beida was the fact that education was free. Students were given a stipend of 19.50 yuan per month, which was equivalent to the monthly salary in an entry-level job. Furthermore, students did not have to pay for food, lodging and books. College education in the Philippines, by contrast, was expensive, especially in private schools.

Despite our hosts extolling the school's progress, we could

not help but notice a number of problems. Teaching materials were rudimentary. Textbooks were mostly stenciled on sheets of poor-quality paper that were stapled together, not bound. We were told that the books were still unfinished, merely drafts that teachers and students were still reviewing. We visited the school library, which at that time was still fronted by the enormous statue of Mao. The library boasted a collection of two million volumes, but those books were locked away and unavailable for anyone to read. I saw a few foreign language journals on display but was told these were available only "for reference."

The classrooms were clean but decrepit and poorly lit. Except for the Maoist slogans painted in red on the walls, corridors were bare and badly in need of paint. At the dormitory of the International Politics Department, students slept in bunk beds, six or more people to a room. If Peking University was indeed the exemplar of the country's education progress, we concluded, then China must be extremely poor.

Before we ended our visit, our hosts took us to an outdoor basketball court to watch varsity teams do scrimmage plays. Hearing that Filipinos loved the sport, they invited us to join their players on the court. Four of us gamely dribbled and shot baskets for several minutes, excited to have some activity, even though we didn't have the proper footwear. As our hosts said, it was all in the spirit of Chairman Mao's edict, "friendship first, competition second." After all that physical exertion, I was so exhausted when we bade goodbye, I couldn't even remember the game's score. But I do recall wondering: what would it be like to study in this peculiar university? I didn't dwell on the idea because it wasn't a realistic question at the time. I expected to be traveling back to the Philippines in just a few days' time. But, six years later, in 1977, I still had not left China and, more importantly, I was enrolled as a student at Peking University.

3

No Exit

How did I get to China? And how did I get stuck there? The answer to the first question involves Henry Kissinger and Zhou Enlai. The answer to the second is more complicated and has less to do with the People's Republic of China than with troubling developments in my homeland, the Philippines.

In July 1971, just a month before we were invited to tour China, Zhou Enlai had hosted a visit of Henry Kissinger, the chief foreign policy adviser to the U.S. President Richard Nixon. Feigning illness while visiting Pakistan, Kissinger secretly flew to Beijing in a Chinese aircraft to negotiate details of a landmark visit. It was a tactical move on America's part to outflank the other Communist giant, the Soviet Union, in the Cold War. Premier Zhou, for his part, wanted to signal to the world, to the Chinese people, and to the various factions in his country that the xenophobic isolation imposed by the Cultural Revolution was coming to an end. The two days of talks between Kissinger and Zhou were a success, and on July 15, Nixon announced that he would make his historic flight to Beijing in February 1972. Chairman Mao, the demi-god of the Communist movement, would meet with U.S. President Richard Nixon, the arch anti-communist leader of the Free World.

It was a startling turn of events. For the U.S., the rapprochement was aimed at checking the Soviet Union's expansionist threats to the U.S. and its allies in Europe. For China, it was an opportunity to break out of diplomatic isolation and ease the military menace posed by the Soviet Union, with which there had been border skirmishes in 1969.

Part of Zhou's diplomatic reopening to the world involved not just high-level contacts with U.S. officials but with "youth delegations." So why shouldn't China then invite one from the Philippines, a staunch U.S. ally in Southeast Asia? That would help reset the geopolitical tone of the times.

The Chinese People's Association for Friendship with Foreign Countries, known as Youxie in Chinese, sent an invitation to the Movement for a Democratic Philippines (MDP), an umbrella organization of a dozen youth and student groups, including the League of Editors for A Democratic Society (LEADS), a group of college editors that I chaired. The China Friendship Association offered to pay for the airfares and expenses for a study tour of China for fifteen people from the Philippines.

Why did they extend an invitation to our fifteen-member Philippine Youth Delegation? I never asked our hosts, but obviously they took us in as a friendly group from a Third World country. When we first arrived in Beijing, the Chinese were also hosting tour groups from Japan, Denmark, Switzerland, Hong Kong and the United States, among others. It was a sign of the times, and I surmised that they expected us, after the tour, to relay the message back home that China had moved on from the chaos of the Cultural Revolution, that it was a safe travel destination and that its doors were again open for exchanges with the "outside world." Our Chinese hosts were certainly keen to show us the best they had to project the image of China as an emerging model of socialism.

It wasn't difficult to find young Filipinos interested in

traveling to the People's Republic. The Philippines was caught up in the same social and political ferment that was sweeping much of the West in the late 1960s and early 1970s: just as John Lennon wore a Mao button in New York City, many Philippine activists saw in Communist China an alternative to the status quo in their own country. I was in my senior year and the outgoing editor-in-chief of the student newspaper at the Philippine College of Commerce. Later renamed the Polytechnic University of the Philippines, it was one of the hotbeds of anti-government activism. I was also an officer of the MDP—and was determined to be one of the fifteen that would get to go to China.

Growing up as a child in a middle-class family in the Philippines, my image of China was mostly associated with food. Chinese immigrants had brought their cuisine with them to the islands over the course of several centuries, among them what we called *pancit Canton* (fried noodles), *pancit mami* (noodle soup), *siopao* (barbecue pork bun) and *lumpiang Shanghai* (fried spring rolls). The Fujian names of many of the Chinese dishes reflected their origin in that coastal province of China. These delicacies were sold in Chinese restaurants in our town and in Manila's Chinatown. On Chinese New Year, Chinese friends would give us gifts of *tikoy*—a sweetened sticky rice cake. But beyond food and Chinese family friends (many of whom were at least a generation removed from their ancestral roots), China was a virtual blank, a distant blurry place.

Of course, I had learned the basics about China in school: it was a sprawling country with a long history, it had invented paper, gunpowder, and the compass. It had a Great Wall. But apart from these clichéd snippets of information, China's image for us was mostly a reflection of what appeared in the Western, anti-communist media: undesirable and negative. My father was a loyal subscriber of TIME, National Geographic and Readers'

Digest magazines. Images of China in these publications in the 1950s and 1960s typically depicted a poor country of starving people under the ruthless Red Chinese rule: emaciated farmers toiling in barren fields, the angry Red Guards and devious leaders. There were terrible rumors of what happened to people who died in the labor camps. Their bones, we were told, were dehydrated, ground and combined into MSG, which was then sprinkled on food. That was the kind of paranoia that Communist China inspired.

In 1969, my eldest sister Nieva visited Hong Kong and Macau — which were then ruled by Britain and Portugal, respectively. She brought back snapshots and impressions of the Red China she had glimpsed with binoculars across the Macau border. Today, that would be the equivalent of a tourist looking into North Korea through binoculars from Dandong city in northeast China.

Then, when I was in college, in the summer of 1970, I attended a forum at the University of the Philippines featuring Orly Mercado, a popular TV anchor, and Charito Planas, a political activist and entrepreneur, who had just travelled to China. They talked about the people's communes, the Red Guards, the Children's Palace, the women militia, the streets full of cyclists. It was exotic and idealistic and enticing to a young, politically curious young man like me, committed to changing his own country. Later that year, some Filipino activists brought back home a copy of *The East Is Red*, a two-hour long Chinese documentary. It was a film version of the song-and-dance extravaganza performed on stage by China's best singers and dancers, telling the history of China's communist revolution. It was a controversial film to screen, given the anti-Communist rhetoric of the Philippine government. The authorities tried to ban it, but some schools defied the ban. I watched it in a half-empty auditorium, sultry because there was no air-conditioning. The high-pitched songs and the pounding of the gongs and drums were stultifying and weird. I fell asleep mid-way through the movie.

Yet, when the opportunity arose to go to China with the Friendship Association, I knew I had to make the trip. The make-up of the fifteen changed as we planned, and we kept our intentions quiet for fear of the military or the police stopping us. The government of Ferdinand Marcos saw me and the people who made up the MDP as "radical students" or worse, because we openly criticized his policies, organized protests against the U.S.-led Vietnam War, and agitated for social and political reforms. We supported impoverished Filipino farmers' demands for land reform. We exposed cases of graft and corruption involving Marcos, his family and his cronies. Many of us had participated in protest rallies, had written anti-government essays and editorials, and had supported labor strikes. We championed academic freedom, as well as the freedom of speech and association, liberties we believed the Marcos administration was hampering with police action and surveillance. I was certain that I was on some government watch-list, as were other members of the group that would be the delegation to China. Among the final fifteen chosen were student leaders, college journalists, feminist activists, a young university professor, a professional reporter, a Benedictine monk and a youth leader from the predominantly Muslim southern region of the Philippines.

Traveling to China would not be simple. There were no formal diplomatic relations between the Philippines and China. Technically, it was illegal for Filipinos to travel into the giant communist nation situated north of us across the South China Sea. Philippine passports were stamped with a specific warning that the documents were "not valid for travel to China, the Soviet Union and other communist countries." To avoid raising suspicions — and being prevented from leaving the Philippines — we decided to split into two groups to fly out of Manila.

When I left home on August 20, 1971, I didn't even get to say goodbye to my father, Cenon. He was the deputy general manager of a government research agency and, on that day, was on a business trip in the Visayas, in central Philippines. I did not think much of it at the time. After all, I thought I was going to be back in three weeks.

I was also exhausted. For nearly a week, I had been campaigning feverishly for the post of vice-president of the Student Council of Polytechnic University of the Philippines, a state university. The students took politics seriously. We formed a leftist bloc of candidates lined up against a "moderate" ticket of candidates. Teams of students from both sides printed campaign leaflets and put up posters and banners in support of their particular candidates. We organized teach-ins, going from classroom to classroom to speak to students and to answer their questions in the quest to win their votes.

On August 19, the eve of the elections, the two competing parties held their final campaign rallies in the college quadrangle. By the time I made it home, about one and a half hours drive from school, I was tired and drained and had lost my voice. It was nearly midnight, but my mother Lourdes was still awake, waiting for me.

She knew I was leaving for China the next day.

"Please wake me up early," I whispered hoarsely. "Really early, like 6 a.m. I need to stop by the school to vote before I catch a noon flight."

Years later, my mother would recall how the next morning she paced in front of my bed. "I agonized whether or not to wake you up," she said. "I had a foreboding that something was amiss." I was sleeping like a log, but she knew I keenly wanted to make the trip. She woke me, reluctantly. I got up, ate breakfast, and packed my luggage.

My mother handed me the equivalent of US$100 for unexpected expenses, even though I told her I'd be taking my personal savings and the Chinese government was covering all costs. I hugged her tightly and said goodbye. I wouldn't see her again for seven years.

On the way to the airport, I stopped by my school to cast my vote for myself and the other candidates running on our party slate. I learned much later that I had won. By then, however, I could no longer go back to assume the post

On the morning of August 20, I flew out of the Manila International Airport aboard a Cathay Pacific flight bound for Hong Kong, our transit destination. It was still a British possession (it would not be returned to China until 1997), and because London and Beijing had diplomatic ties, the colony was an entry point for many foreigners into the Communist mainland. There I met up with fourteen other Filipino youth leaders who would comprise what our Chinese hosts would call the "Philippine Youth Delegation".

Months earlier, at least two groups of business executives and journalists had visited China and publicly talked about their trips without getting into trouble with the authorities. Still, they were illegal travels under Philippine law at that time. We were prepared for the possible consequences. After all, we thought, the Philippines was supposed to be a model of American brand of democracy and freedom in Asia, even though we could already see signs of repression under the administration of Ferdinand Marcos. We could always resort to legal means and, with the help of good lawyers, assert our rights to travel and engage in academic inquiry. We were so confident we even gave an interview with a Philippine journalist in Hong Kong, who wrote a report about our China journey, along with all our names and affiliation.

On the morning of August 21, 1971, our 15-member "Philippine Youth Delegation" set off by train for what was to be a three-week tour of China. We stopped over in Shenzhen for lunch and proceeded by train to the port-city of Guangzhou, capital of Guangdong province. After a quick city tour, we flew to Beijing. When the two-propeller Tupolev plane touched down at the Peking airport the evening of August 21, I pumped my fist — furtively — felling like an astronaut who had just landed on the moon.

As I waited to disembark with scores of fellow travelers, I could virtually hear in my ears the triumphant refrain of the Beatles song "Magical Mystery Tour." I started to imagine what I'd see and experience in the inscrutable "Red China," as the People's Republic was commonly then known. I thought I would explore the place, snap souvenir photos, collect vignettes, and then take the plane back home and pick up where I had left off: fighting the looming dictatorship in the Philippines. I had no idea that I was instead about to embark on a surreal and extremely protracted journey.

We were greeted by a phalanx of gray-haired Chinese officials and ruddy-cheeked Red Guards. Waving copies of the Little Red Book of Chairman Mao's quotations, they shouted slogans hailing China-Philippines friendship and professing support for the oppressed peoples of the world. We responded with inspired rendition in Filipino of Bayan Ko (My Motherland), a Philippine patriotic hymn, and the Internationale.

We shook hands with the Red Guards like we were long-lost comrades. In fact, we looked like youths from different planets. My hippie-inspired hairdo was nearly as long as the bobbed hair of the female Red Guards. My attire — a striped shirt, bell-bottom pants and a pair of Ray-Ban sunglasses—juxtaposed starkly with their white cotton shirts, baggy pants and ubiquitous Mao badges pinned on their shirts.

In the first few days of our China jaunt, we visited must-see tourist destinations—Tiananmen Square, the Forbidden City, the Great Wall— totally oblivious of what was going on in the Philippines.

As we traveled further into the country to meet Chinese university students and representatives of the Red Guards, our Friendship Association hosts called for an emergency meeting. They had heard of disturbing reports from the Philippines. On August 21, the same day we entered China, a bombing incident disrupted a political rally in Manila. No details were available, but they promised to get Philippine newspapers shipped from Hong Kong,

Even as we took in the sights around Beijing, we were anxious for news from home. What was happening in Manila? What could be the consequences for left-leaning activists like us? Information was hard to come by: there were no English language papers or magazines available. We could not even make overseas calls from Beijing to reach our family and friends because the two countries had no ties and so there were no telecommunications links. There was certainly no Philippine embassy we could walk into to ask for updates.

A few days later, our hosts brought in back issues of Philippine newspapers from Hong Kong. What those publications reported wasn't good: hundreds of people back home had been arrested, including many student leaders we knew.

As days turned to weeks, we realized that the political situation in Manila would not favor our return any time soon. Were any of us on the Marcos government blacklist? Which ones among us could return without fear of arrest and penalty, and which of us could not?

Our Chinese hosts advised us to be patient as we waited for more news from home. They generously offered to continue covering our food and lodging in Beijing, but we grew frustrated with the uncertainty, and balked at the confines of our hotel. All we could do was walk to the cafeteria, eat, then walk back to our rooms. Our hosts arranged for additional activities to keep us occupied — we visited more schools, as well as communes, kindergartens, and hospitals. They took us out to swim, play basketball, and see Peking opera or the ballet — anything to keep us busy or distracted. But we were strangers in a strange land, unable to speak the language, completely beholden to our hosts, and extremely homesick.

After weeks of inquiries, we learned that I and four other members of the group were on the government's list of people to be arrested upon arrival in Manila. In October, eight members of the group who were not on the blacklist decided to fly home via Tokyo, instead of Hong Kong, to avoid police detection. Later, some of them managed to write to us to say they had been spotted on arrival at the airport and interrogated, but because their families had hired lawyers, they were allowed to re-enter the country as long as they promised to appear in court if summoned by the government. A month later, the other two colleagues not on the wanted list flew home too. Five of us remained, knowing we could not go home without facing jail. It was a terrible realization.

We envied our friends who had been able to leave China to be reunited with their families back home. Yet home would not prove to be secure for them. On September 21, 1972, Marcos imposed martial law in the Philippines, and many of them were arrested. Some were tortured. One of the original fifteen who came with me to China, a Benedictine monk named Carlos Tayag, was among many who were referred as "desaparecidos" — or the disappeared. Those who evaded imprisonment went underground or found a way to slip out of the country. By the time all that news trickled back to me, two years later, my Philippine passport had expired. I was stateless in China.

The five of us who remained realized that if we were to survive an indefinite stay in China, we had to learn to speak Mandarin Chinese. I had given myself an early start. I had been intrigued by the language ever since we entered the country in August 1971 and I learned a few words on the train from Hong Kong to China's southern border where we walked across the Luohu bridge into Shenzhen—which was then a sleepy fishing village. A few decades later, it would become the factory of the world, a showcase of China's economic transformation begun under Deng Xiaoping. Our China Travel Service guide, who spoke fluent English, taught me a few phrases—*ni hao* (Hello!) and *zhongfei youyi wansui* (Long live the friendship between China and the Philippines!). He explained how each character in Chinese had to be pronounced with a specific tone to differentiate it from other words with the same sound. It seemed complicated, but it did not deter me from reciting the phrases repeatedly and even using them when I met people during the tour.

During our first three weeks in China, I constantly asked the English-speaking guides to teach me a few more words. I learned to say *"Ni jiao shenme mingzi?"* —What's your name?—and *"Wo jiao Ji Mi"* —My name is Jimi. I learned to sing Chinese songs including The East is Red—a paean to Chairman Mao—and The Peoples of the World Will Surely Win—a Cultural Revolution song predicting the collapse of American Imperialism. Working to master the songs increased my obsession with the language and complemented my efforts to learning more phrases. I also started scribbling and pairing off Chinese written characters. It was like being a five-year old again, discovering Lego and working out how everything could fit together. It was challenging, frustrating, and gratifying all at the same time. The five of us asked our hosts if we could enroll in a local school to learn Chinese in a formal classroom setting, but we were told it was not possible. Most universities had been shuttered during the Cultural Revolution, and while some, including Beida, had recently reopened, they were not accepting foreign students. That depressed us. Not only were we trapped in a foreign country, we also couldn't even go to school to learn its language.

So I continued to learn the language on my own, mostly by talking to our guides and, whenever I had a chance, chatting with a few of the older hotel attendants, some of whom spoke English fluently. Unlike the guides, who were much younger, these hotel workers were of the generation that would have been stigmatized for having the bourgeois ability to speak a foreign tongue. They would have been persecuted for being one of the so-called "*chou laojiu*", the Stinking Ninth Category, which meant the intellectuals who were denounced at the height of the Cultural Revolution as being one of the exploitative classes (the other eight were landlords, rich farmers, counterrevolutionaries, bad influences, right-wingers, traitors, spies, and capitalist roaders). They were lucky to have landed a job as a hotel attendant; most of their peers were probably still doing hard labor in the countryside.

I also befriended a few younger hotel attendants who were keen to learn English. The times were changing and with the coming visit of the American president, there was a "English craze" among young urban Chinese. I would chat with them in English, teach them words and phrases in exchange for Chinese words and phrases. It was also a way of flirting with the pretty, rosy-cheeked girls who worked at the hotel.

However, our lives in spartan hotel rooms continued to be painfully boring. And the temperature in Beijing was getting to be bitterly cold. We Filipinos are not accustomed to winter because our country lies just above the equator.

In the first weeks and months, I stewed in homesickness because I refused to abandon the fading hope of going home. Getting suddenly stranded in China was brutal but coping with uncertainty was worse. My fellow exiles and I did not know it was going to take twelve years. We kept thinking, "maybe next week", then, "well, maybe next month." Winter turned to spring, and spring to summer. We still could not go home. It was one disappointment after another.

Perhaps the most bruising part of my exile life was the wrenching boredom and dearth of information and recreation. For years, I endured isolation and monotony. Everywhere I turned was incessant propaganda. In newspapers and magazines, billboards and street signs, radio and television, movie houses and theaters, in barbershops and hotel lobbies, the mind-numbing message was the omniscience of Chairman Mao and the Communist Party.

This quirk of fate became a turning point for me. It was a start of a life-changing adventure. In a sense, my exile gave me a rare chance to be an eyewitness to the historic transformation of China and helped me become a "China-watcher".

To cope with exile life, I shook off negative thoughts and looked at my predicament philosophically. I began to treat the experience as a rare opportunity to know China firsthand. While on one level, my forced exile in China interrupted my youth, on another, it opened new paths for me to pursue. I had to give up my college education and a comfortable middle-class lifestyle. I had to forego a life that, even if imperfect and frustrating, allowed for free thinking, association and spontaneity—the singing and dancing, the wit and humor and the outdoor life that youths of my age and background enjoyed back home. I also had to end the political and social activism that gave me a sense of purpose beyond just acquiring a college diploma. Most important, I was forced to live away from my family and friends, whom I missed terribly. I especially missed my mother's delicious home cooking.

Struggling with all these issues, my compatriots and I told our Chinese hosts that we wanted to earn our keep. We wanted to work. They suggested that we go to the countryside just as many young Chinese had done since the Cultural Revolution began. They would arrange everything for us. We agreed, even though we had heard whispers of how difficult that existence could be. When our hosts told us we would be going to Hunan, we were elated. It was not only Chairman Mao's home province but, when we pulled out our maps to figure out where it was, we decided the climate there would be much more pleasant because it was far to the south of cold Beijing.

We were wrong. We arrived in central Hunan province in December 1971, a few days before New Year's Eve, in the middle of a snowstorm. We were taken to the Xiangjiang State Farm in Hengyang County, which would be our home for many months to come. Unlike Beijing, all of the buildings and houses in Xiangjiang did not have indoor heating, and to ward off the cold, we had to wear several layers of clothing, including cotton-padded pants and jackets. To boil drinking water and warm up our dormitory, we had to learn to light a primitive stove with firewood and briquettes. Wearing multilayered, bulky clothing posed a challenge in itself, and using the farm's communal latrines while wearing them was even worse. One sight that will never leave my mind was of the white maggots crawling on the mud-packed latrine walls.

Later, I learned to balance on my shoulders a bamboo pole

hooked on both ends with wooden buckets full of human waste, and we carried the fertilizer from the latrines to our own vegetable plots.

In spite of the hardships and primitive conditions, we fired ourselves up with the romantic notion that we were participating in a noble socialist experiment and getting a close-up look at life in China's revolutionary countryside. Xiangjiang State Farm was a modest enterprise that had rice fields and orchards as well as a small tea plantation. The hundred or so families there also raised pigs, chicken, goats, and other animals. We were assigned to work with a team of farmers, and sometimes with young people who formed the area's militia. We planted and harvested rice when it was in season, picked tea leaves, dug ditches, and repaired roads. Occasionally, we would labor side by side with a batch of seventy to eighty high school graduates who had been sent down on the farm to "learn from the farmers," just as we were doing. The Cultural Revolution was deeply entrenched throughout every corner of China, not just in the cities and universities.

But the romance of working for the revolution and learning from the peasants wore off after a few weeks. I found the manual labor onerous because I had grown up in the suburbs of Manila in a middle-class family. My parents both worked as senior managers in government agencies, and my five siblings and I led comfortable lives. We had a family car and two live-in household helpers. I hardly had chores, except on weekends, when my father would assign us to plant or prune trees in our garden or wash the car.

Work was hard in Xiangjiang. Passing time after work was just as hard. After sweating in the fields, we had to face stifling ennui. There was little else to do. The farm had practically nothing to read in English, just a couple of old magazines and a few propaganda pamphlets hailing the glorious achievements of the New China. None of us cared much for the local cuisine, which was for the most part extremely spicy, and made up of fermented tofu, fatty pork and pickled vegetables. Our repeated requests to dial down the spice level fell on deaf ears. Our cook, an elderly comrade, would not prepare any dishes without throwing in a handful of tongue-numbing *lajiao* (chilies) and *hujiao* (peppers). Even an omelet had to be hot and spicy.

We killed time playing basketball and ping pong. I also took many cold showers. As foreigners, we were not allowed to socialize or fraternize with the female farmers and cadres, nor with the girls among the urban youth who were assigned to the farm.

I missed my family and friends terribly. Writing letters home was of little consolation. I could not tell my parents that I was working on a farm, because they might conclude that their poor son had been banished to a gulag and had become a prisoner of the Chinese Communists. So, in the few letters that I sent to them via third countries like the U.S. and Canada, I just said that I was in good health and getting daily exercise. I said I was learning a lot about agriculture. But I always told them how much I missed them.

My loneliness and isolation were compounded because I did not yet speak Mandarin fluently and couldn't begin to communicate properly with my Chinese co-workers. I went out of my way to try to have conversations with the people around me, but I was often stumped by the local accents. Older co-workers in the Xiangjiang State Farm spoke thick Hunanese Chinese, which was how Chairman Mao spoke. But younger ones were able to converse to varying degrees in Mandarin— *putonghua*—which was what I had been picking up before going to the countryside.

Fitting in was a struggle. My long hair, bell-bottom pants, striped Orlon T-shirt, and the Ray-Ban dark glasses clashed with the de rigueur proletarian look. One by one, I had to let them go. After a few months, I gave in to wearing crew-cut hair, monochromatic Mao jackets and baggy pants. I got comfortable with the new working-class look, and in winter, the long johns, cotton-padded pants and overcoat, turned me into a big, inflated ball.

I never stopped trying to learn the language. We were provided with some help by our hosts in Beijing. Song Mingjiang, a lanky bespectacled native of the coastal city of Tianjin, was assigned by the Foreign Ministry to serve as translator and, significantly, as a Chinese language instructor for our group. For the first three months of our stay, Song Laoshi—Teacher Song—lived with us on the farm. In the mornings, he would join us in laboring in the fields and the roads; then, for two or three hours in the afternoons, he taught us intensive elementary Chinese.

We didn't really have a textbook, just exercises mimeographed on rice paper. Lesson 1 was made up of drills on the basics: "My name is xxx", and "Please drink tea.". It also taught us how to say, "I live in Rawalpindi." The lessons were probably originally produced for Pakistani pilots in China to learn to fly military aircraft.

Song had learned English at the Beijing Foreign Languages Institute, China's premier training ground for diplomats, interpreters and linguists, and he spoke the language with a British accent. Before he joined the Foreign Ministry, he had taught Mandarin to foreign students at the Institute which, like almost all schools in China, was shut down when the Cultural Revolution started in 1966. It was still closed when he was with us in Xiangjiang.

Learning Mandarin from Song was both a torture and a treat.

In the beginning, I found him intimidating and exacting. Like an officer in a boot camp, he would have me repeat words again and again in a ferocious drill until I got the pronunciation and tones just right. He would then ask me to form sentences using new words that I barely understood. Yet all of his strictness was delivered in a loud but musical baritone, enunciating each word in melodic ways.

I struggled with Chinese tones and grammar. After a month of this formal instruction, I was close to giving up. But Teacher Song was patient and encouraging. After class he would invite me to his room and answered my questions. He would then regale me with stories, anecdotes and trivia about China and its history and culture. He told me about the huge funeral tumulus in Xi'an, an ancient city west of Beijing, where the body of China's first Emperor, Qin Shihuang, is believed to be entombed, and where priceless funerary objects were buried. He could recite Tang dynasty poetry by heart. He could perform the Tianjin version of *kuaibanr*, a comic monologue style akin to rap. He also shared tales and insights into the Cultural Revolution — hinting that while it may have been well-intentioned, it was excessive. He said China needed to move on. He spoke admiringly of Zhou Enlai, and of the Premier's diplomatic and people skills.

Teacher Song also taught me a few Chinese songs, including parts of arias from "Taking Tiger Mountain by Strategem," one of the eight opera productions approved by Mao's wife, Jiang Qing, who was also the country's culture czar. I persisted in struggling to master Chinese for a few more weeks; and then, one day, I woke up and realized that I could understand and speak the language. Somehow, all the work had pushed me over the threshold of the Chinese language. I had broken through!

Teacher Song left the farm in the spring of 1972 to return to Beijing and the diplomatic corps, which like many institutions had been battered by the Cultural Revolution. Premier Zhou was then rebuilding it. I don't know if Song's teaching stint in Xiangjiang contributed to his advancement, but his career would later blossom, and he retired in the 1990s after serving as China's ambassador to the European Union.

By the summer of 1972, our time at the Hunan state farm was up and my fellow exiles and I were reassigned to a fishing corporation in Yantai, Shandong Province, an overnight train ride south from Beijing. Yantai was a charming and underdeveloped port city at the time. It was also very cold. But the food there better suited our tastes than the spicy Hunan dishes we had been forced to eat at the farm.

On board Yantai's trawlers, we would sail out for five to seven days at a turn. Working alongside Chinese members of the crew, I dropped and pulled in huge fishing nets and learned to navigate the boats. I shoveled fish from the nets into refrigerated containers in the ship's belly. The trips took us to the far reaches of the East China Sea near the Korean Peninsula as well as areas farther south, close to Shanghai. At the end of a working day, we typically weighed anchor in the high seas and had nothing else to do except talk, play cards, and sleep. By then, my Mandarin had significantly improved and I was able to converse with my Chinese co-workers.

One night after a long day of work, as our trawler ship anchored in the East China Sea, I decided to use the spare time to read the *People's Daily*, the official newspaper of the Communist Party, and to practice writing the Chinese characters that I had just learned. It was a tedious, mind-numbing exercise but a welcome respite from the physical labor. I also had a few Chinese magazines and novels and while others slept, I read voraciously to improve my grasp of the language.

Most of my co-workers had gone to bed. My two bunkmates

were soundly sleeping. I slipped under my cotton-padded quilt and sat up in my 2x1 meter cubicle bed, reading under a faintly lit wall lamp. I peered through the porthole. It was nearly pitch dark. I saw a borderless body of water. I could hear the faint, rhythmic sounds of waves lapping at the boat, punctuated by the snores of my bunkmates. I first felt a tug of ennui, then homesickness. I thought of my family back home, who must miss me as much as I missed them. I thought of my Mom. I imagined her, standing at the porch of our home, smiling, as she waited to usher me back home. She must be worried to death about what may have happened to me. I thought of my friends and college contemporaries in the Philippines, wondering how they were doing in the face of the ruthless political repression under Martial Law. I thought of my girlfriend Jo-Ann Maglipon, editor of the college paper of Maryknoll, an exclusive Catholic college for girls. She may have been one of the hundreds of anti-government activists arrested after the military crackdown in the Philippines a few months earlier.

Then I thought of my own fate. When would I ever be able to go home? Time in the trawler boat moved slowly, and the chances of me being able to go home were fast disappearing. What was I doing in China, wasting my time doing things that had no relevance or use for my future, or for the people back home? Why was I even learning this pesky Chinese language? Was I not going home soon anyway? I started to tear up, and then broke into soft, desperate sobs. I realized it was the first time I had cried over my plight. I quickly took control of my emotions. My comrades should not see me crying. We were all expected to be "grim and determined," as radical student leaders put it.

To make more progress on my Chinese, I borrowed a blue, two-inch-thick English-Chinese dictionary, a special compendium of commonly used terms and phrases. It belonged to a translator friend and was issued only to interpreters and cadres involved in foreign affairs and education. It was not available in bookstores. An expanded political glossary, it was sprinkled with Maoist slogans and the arcane ideological vocabulary of the Cultural Revolution. Many of the phrases are no longer in use, but because of their relevance during the politically fraught 1970s, they were then important to know by heart. I copied the dictionary's entries by hand, character by character, and memorized their English translations. After a year, when I had copied almost one-third of the entries into three thick notebooks, the time came to return it to my friend. He was so moved by my efforts to master his language that he gave it to me as a gift.

It was a grueling process, but in the end, learning Chinese provided me with many opportunities.

4

FAKE FOREIGNER

I COULD PASS FOR a Chinese. I could squat like a farmhand, ungainly and low to the ground, legs spiking from the hips like a grasshopper — just like my co-workers in the Hunan countryside where I toiled for more than a year. I carried my clothes and belongings in an olive-green satchel like the foot soldiers of the People's Liberation Army. I smoked a pack-a-day of Zhengzhou, a cheap brand of cigarette also from Hunan, the birthplace of China's paramount chain smoker and then-living god, Chairman Mao Zedong. In between puffs, I would hold the lit stick like a peasant — not elegantly between the index and middle fingers, but between my thumb and forefinger. I spoke fluent enough Putonghua — that's Mandarin to foreigners — and could read more than 800 characters, which put me on par with some rural Chinese, many of whom were still haphazardly educated.

If people in Beijing suspected I was out of place, they probably explained me away as a bumpkin cadre.

It was the summer of 1974, a critical moment in Mao's cataclysmic Cultural Revolution, when peasants were hailed as heroes and intellectuals were little better than scum. I'd returned to the capital after nearly three years away, first in the agricultural collective in Hunan and then on fishing boats on the Yellow Sea off Shandong province. It was an internal exile not unlike that experienced by young Chinese sent off to farms and faraway communes to be cleansed of their bourgeois inclinations. I was young too, just twenty-three, and confident I knew how to survive in China.

But I passed only as long as no one dug deep into my satchel to find the expensive watch—a Girard Perregaux that my parents gave me when I graduated high school six years earlier—or a pair of bell-bottom jeans, which were then fashionable in the West and would have betrayed an extraterritorial decadence. The watch and trousers were mementoes from my homeland. As was my passport, which identified me as Jaime A. FlorCruz, a name not out of place in the Philippines—for three centuries Spain's Asian outpost—but alien in the People's Republic. I'd been stuck in China since August 1971.

My passport was useless as a get-out-of-China card. The Manila government had banned me from returning home with the threat of arrest for leftist college political activity—among which was the trip that took me to the People's Republic.

I despaired of ever seeing my parents and my country again. But even as I yearned for the Philippines, I resigned myself to making China stand-in for home, absorbing its language, traditions, songs, poetry, history, politics, and the way ordinary people navigated through extraordinary, often perilous, times. My aim was to transform adversity into opportunity.

The great game of ruling China is played out behind the walls of Zhongnanhai, adjacent to the old Imperial City and the cluster of villas in its vicinity. Since 1966—and with Mao's blessing—the upper hand belonged to hardline ideologues who wanted to level Chinese society and create an egalitarian paradise. But by 1973, even they conceded that the economy was on the verge of collapse. That allowed for the return—also with Mao's blessing—of purged pragmatists like Deng Xiaoping who knew how to prevent that kind of catastrophe. In 1974, the political balance of power had shifted enough that even people in the faraway countryside could sense a difference. Among the consequences, elite schools shut for years by the militant Red Guard were gradually allowed to reopen. That year, the Beijing Languages Institute—where Teacher Song had learned English—reopened and was again accepting foreign students. It was again the premier training ground for overseas students in Chinese language, and Chinese students in foreign languages.

If China was to be my home, I couldn't just get along with the 800 characters I had learned with a kindly tutor in Hunan. I had to master the language more fully. The Institute would certify that, and its imprimatur would allow me to seek admission to the country's best universities as they came back to life. I asked my Chinese hosts and patrons from the China Friendship Association for permission to apply. Permission was granted and, more importantly, I was accepted.

I was fairly fluent in Mandarin by the time I enrolled in the fall of 1974 and was placed in a special advanced class with overseas Chinese who had come to the mainland to polish their skills. With the head start I'd made in the countryside, the school told me I could finish the three-year degree in Mandarin Chinese and translation in two years. The timing would be perfect. The Language Institute degree would come at the right moment to later qualify me for admission to Peking University and join Beida's remarkable Class of '77.

The Languages Institute was a revelation, and a reminder of the world beyond China. I shared classes and dormitory rooms with students from every continent. I made friends with students from Albania, North Vietnam, Laos, Sri Lanka, Gabon, Sierra Leone, Ethiopia and Palestine; with them, I conversed in a new common language, Mandarin. I gravitated towards those from countries that spoke English, happy to use a familiar language. I caught up with the "outside world" after having been isolated in China for so long. Some lent me newspapers, magazines and books they'd brought with them. Others passed on cassette tapes of songs and music. That's how I discovered The Jackson 5, Boney M and Elton John. I felt like Rip Van Winkle waking from his stupor.

There were more than new friendships. I had a brief romance with one schoolmate, a girl from the UK, but it broke off when she decided to go home after a year's study. All my new non-Chinese friends did the same: they weren't there to earn a Chinese degree, and most went home after a few months. I'd go to the Beijing airport or the local train station to see them off. And, with each farewell, I felt left behind. Do I have to make friends all over again? Maybe I should find a girlfriend who can't leave? A Chinese girlfriend?

Or maybe not.

The Chinese government officially "discouraged" (read: forbid) its citizens from dating, much less marrying, foreigners — even one who could pass for Chinese. In the 1950s and '60s, only a few intermarriages were sanctioned, and had to be approved by no less than Premier Zhou Enlai. Through most of the Cultural Revolution, which lasted from 1966 to 1976, it was completely taboo. Chinese girls who dared to fraternize with foreigners were ostracized. In the worst cases, they were branded *liumang* ("hooligans" or "sluts") and banished to internment camps for one or two years of "reeducation" (read: hard labor).

But then Hai Ou (Chinese for "Seagull") caught my eye. Or did I catch hers? It was August 1975. She was with her family at a table in a restaurant in *Wudaokou*, a neighborhood next to the BLI campus. I was celebrating a classmate's birthday at the same place. She wore no makeup and was dressed like almost every woman in China — faded army jacket, blue baggy pants, and cotton shoes. She braided her hair in pigtails and tied the ends with red strings. Her bangs rested just above the well-defined eyebrows of her extraordinary face. It was the shape the Chinese call *guazilian* — sunflower seed — where the sharper end is the chin, the kind of oval possessed by the youthful Elizabeth Taylor and Naomi Campbell. Hai Ou's was poised gracefully on a ballerina neck.

I couldn't keep my eyes off her. She noticed, glanced back, and smiled.

It turned out, after I inquired with the restaurant staff, that she was distantly related to our waiter, who explained that her father had relocated the family to Beijing to teach Japanese at BLI after living abroad. They were returned overseas Chinese, a class of patriotic citizens who enjoyed special privileges because they'd given up the material benefits of the capitalist world to help rebuild the Motherland. She lived with her parents on campus and attended a local high school a few bus stops away.

As Hai Ou and her family finished their meal and walked out, the waiter introduced them to our group — and, specifically, Hai Ou to me. She complimented my Chinese and I hinted I could help her with English. I asked her if we could meet again off-campus. Maybe tomorrow at the Summer Palace, an ornate Qing dynasty pleasure ground that was now a public park?

"That's not a convenient time," she whispered. But, she continued, she was visiting an uncle convalescing in the Beijing No. 3 Hospital, a bus stop away from BLI. "You want to meet there, if you're free?"

Of course, I was free.

Thus, we had our first date, seated on a long bench next to other patients and visitors, in the corridor of one of Beijing's best hospitals. Speaking in Chinese, I told her my story of being stuck in China. Hai Ou told me hers: born in China, she had lived briefly in Hongkong as a child before her parents decided to return to the "Motherland" — part of a wave of overseas-educated expatriates lured to come home to build the New China. At eighteen, she had adapted quickly to life in the capital and already spoke with a Beijing twang.

She was cautious about being seen alone with me; even though I could be mistaken for Chinese, I was still a *waiguoren* (foreigner). There were prying eyes everywhere: the men and women deputized by every *danwei* — that is, the work unit, the basic organizational block of communist China — to make sure everyone behaved. It was their business to be the busybodies of society, keeping track of who was doing what and reporting their suspicions up the line of the party. The official tattletales of the *danwei* are mostly retired women, known politely as "aunties" or more sinisterly as the *malie laotaitai* (Marxist-Leninist old wives).

Everything interested the ideologically correct and puritanical *malie laotaitai* — especially the sexual behavior of the members of their *danwei*. Young people caught in premarital sex were disciplined. Adults who carried on extramarital affairs were punished. Married couples would walk two or three paces apart and not hold hands in public to avoid attracting misplaced gossip — and potentially troublesome *danwei* reports. And, well, if a romance involved a foreigner, well, that was completely unacceptable in Mao's xenophobic China. By befriending a foreign national, Hai Ou was already defying rules.

We stayed at the hospital till sundown and I walked her back to BLI. Under the cover of darkness, I held her hand and she did not resist. She smiled. We stopped at a sprawling cabbage field, found a corner and sat on the dirt. I kissed her on the cheek. She shifted her eyes, left and right, to make sure no one saw it. It's dark, she whispered, time to head back.

We arranged for our next date in the Summer Palace grounds. We got into a boat in the park's scenic lake and rowed away from the crowds but still in view. Alone with me out in the water, Hai Ou talked about the rigid puritanism of China.

"In my school, girl students are seated in one section and boys on the other," she said. "No one crosses the middle. After class, girls and boys walk home on separate sides of the road. We call it the 38ᵗʰ parallel," referring to the post-war demarcation dividing North and South Korea. "Sometimes, classmates quarrel just because someone's elbow crosses the line. It's ridiculous. If a boy actually tried to touch you, he'd be branded as a *chou liumang* (stinking pervert)."

"It's okay if boys held hands with boys, or girls with girls, but boys with girls—not okay," she said laughing. But she had rules for herself: "I talk to whoever I want to. I guess that makes me a rebel." We stayed out till sunset and promised to meet again.

I knew not to send her flowers or sweets, no love letters, no material evidence that could be presented to the authorities as proof of a liaison. Instead, we met in public places like parks and movie nights. In the Cultural Revolution, films weren't presented in theaters where couples could cuddle in the dark. People gathered in open spaces on school campuses, bringing their own folding stools or benches. They sat in front of an 8-by-12-foot white sheet fastened on two 14-foot poles. A film-projection team would arrive to set up the projector. And when it was dark enough, they'd start the movie out in the open.

One autumn evening in 1975, Language Institute organized a movie night featuring *Juelie* (Rupture), a 90-minute film promoted by Jiang Qing, Mao's wife, who was both culture czarina and the leader of the so-called hardline leftist Gang of Four. Set in a contemporary people's commune, *Juelie* ridiculed Chinese intellectuals, caricaturing an old professor as a clumsy textbook pusher with little understanding of politics and the correct ideology. In contrast, the film glorified the local communist leader and the farmers who followed practical farming methods while they devoutly studied Chairman Mao's teachings.

Hai Ou and I watched the movie while standing side by side, leaning on our bikes. I placed my hand on hers. She looked at me and smiled.

"*Wuliao* (boring)," she whispered. With a slight flick of her head, she signaled it was time to sneak out. The crowd remained glued to the screen.

I followed her lead as we pedaled along the tree-lined, poorly lit streets of *Wudaokou*, then crossed into the next neighborhood, talking and joking about how the movie was so bad it was funny. In the mid-70s, Beijing's streets were silent much of the time. There were tens of thousands of bicycles, of course, but they weren't noisy. The trolleys and state-owned cars contributed some mechanical growls but all that was diminished by night. When the sun went down, silence was interrupted only by the hooves of horses pulling carts carrying vegetables and fruit from suburban communes for sale the next morning in the city's markets. At times, you could hear the tinkling of bells announcing the arrival of a camel caravan coming from the arid north.

But on that night, as we ran away from Jiang Qing's movie, we seemed to be the only ones out on the street. We must have pedaled for half an hour before deciding to turn back. She suggested we stop to rest. We left our bikes on the side of the asphalt road and walked several steps into an apple orchard likely owned by the local commune. A few lamps lit the street, but the orchard was pitch dark. The only sound was the rustle of autumn leaves.

We found a corner under a tree. I offered to set down my Mao jacket as a blanket but she demurred. She took out her cotton handkerchief and offered to wipe my sweaty face. I took the hankie, dabbed my face and pocketed it. We sat on a thicket of fallen leaves. Ripening apples hung above us.

At first we spoke in whispers, lest strangers hear us. But slowly, we got bolder. I asked her to do that welcome dance she and her schoolmates performed to greet important visitors. She stood up, lifted her chin and arms, and, just like a ballerina, spun and pranced while humming the strident music. Then she took my hands and pulled me up. We waltzed and swayed, our eyes focused on each other, our bodies pressing closer. I clutched her head and pressed my lips to hers. She opened her mouth and we kissed some more. I pushed her against the tree.

She was as passionate — and as aroused — as I was. Amid all the kisses her eyes looked left and right, warily. I thought about stopping. Were we pushing our luck? What if we get caught? But my desire for her made me want more. She didn't want to stop. I unbuttoned her jacket, then her cotton blouse. She did not resist, even though she kept her eyes wide open and alert. She pulled my face against her bosom. I could feel her vocal cords vibrating, though she wasn't saying a word. Her heart was beating as I held and kissed her breasts.

A light flashed. Behind us, three men appeared.

"What are you doing here?" barked one, training a flashlight onto our flushed faces.

They were middle-aged men, dressed in well-worn canvas jackets. One of them held what looked like a truncheon. We froze, unable to speak. Hai Ou fumbled trying to button up her jacket. One man grabbed her wrist.

"Keep your hands off me," she said, attempting to walk away. Another man blocked her.

"Who are you?" I mumbled in Mandarin, trying to summon a look of indignation. "What are you doing?"

"We're the militia," an older burly man replied in a deep voice. "You are coming with us."

Virtually every *danwei* (work unit) in China had a militia, a paramilitary detachment, tasked to police their neighborhood, like the apple orchard commune. The two men grabbed Hai Ou's arms and dragged her toward the street where we had left our bikes. She tried wrestling away, shouting expletives.

"You!" the man with a flashlight turned to me. "You go home! Leave!"

"No, no," I protested. Suddenly, all the Mandarin vocabulary that I learned the past several months seemed inadequate. Dumbfounded, I didn't know what else to say, except: "This is not right. This is not good."

I picked up my bike, my knees shaking, starting to move away, confused. Questions flooded my head. What's going on? Why are they letting me go? Why don't they take me too? Did they figure out I was a foreigner? Was it because my bicycle had the kind of black registration plate issued exclusively to foreigners? Or was it the way I looked or spoke Mandarin? Was I not passing for Chinese?

I had started pedaling away, as ordered, then suddenly, the thought arose: I can't leave Hai Ou behind. I did a U-turn and pedaled toward her and the three men. As I got closer, I saw Hai Ou arguing with the men. But noticing my approach, she pointed at me in seeming anger and shrieked in Mandarin: "*Jia waiguoren!* (He's a fake foreigner!)"

One of the men charged in my direction. I pulled the brakes and froze. What the hell was she doing? Why was she saying that? Then I knew what she was trying to tell me: *Turn around and leave!*

I sped away. My mind was racing. Why did she say what she did? I pulled together something of a rationale. If I were a "fake

54

foreigner" – that is, if I were a genuine Chinese citizen – then ours was a less serious case, just that of two immature Chinese caught petting under the apple tree. If I were a real foreigner, then who knows what scandal and personal legal crisis it might start – for both of us. It was totally whacky logic. I looked back a few times, until the four figures standing under the streetlamp blurred and faded.

Anger and guilt and fear fought over me. What's going to happen to Hai Ou? Will she be sent to a labor camp? How did I get myself into this mess?

I would not see Hai Ou again for a long time – and then only fleetingly.

"We Chinese know too little," Hai Ou once said cryptically during one of our dates. Because of her background, she felt the world was big and China small and small-minded.

In the days and weeks and months after our interrupted rendezvous, I knew nothing at all about what happened to her. I had hoped that her relatives or friends might tell me. No one did. I went to her cousin, the waiter, but he said he knew nothing. I didn't know what to do.

I'd been in China long enough to realize that the less the authorities knew, the better. I could not go to the school authorities or to the police to file a complaint or even to inquire about her whereabouts. If they knew what had happened that night, it might make things worse – for me as well as for anyone who knew her and me. Filing a complaint would have meant admitting to a crime – an illicit liaison between an unmarried man and woman, and worse, a Chinese and a foreign national. It was a totalitarian system, after all. One investigation could lead to another and result in a Kafka-esque trial and nightmarish incarceration. And it was also the Cultural Revolution – where political hatreds made everything even more perilous.

I thought of Hai Ou constantly. And of those last words: fake foreigner. They raised so many questions. Yes, I understood that if I were Chinese, making out with her wasn't illegal, just reprehensible; but if she convinced the militia men that she was shouting mad because she'd just realized she'd been seduced into having an affair by a Chinese man pretending to be foreign, did that devalue being Chinese? And wasn't that politically incorrect? Or did she just mean to confuse the militia men? Just as she confused me. I had no answers.

I also had no photograph of Hai Ou. My only memento was the salmon-colored handkerchief I pocketed when we sat under the apple tree after she used it to wipe the sweat off my face. It was folded up and tucked away in my dormitory closet. From time to time, I'd take it out to bring her to mind. That was all I could do as I buried myself in schoolwork.

It was in the hustle and bustle of my first year in *Beida*, during the summer of 1978, that I saw Hai Ou again.

That day I was rushing to a lunch meeting in Beijing's Xinqiao Hotel, which was famous for a restaurant that served Pakistani and Western cuisine. I had just jumped into the hotel elevator when a woman rushed in as well. I immediately recognized her: the doe eyes, fair skin, rosy cheeks, curled lips, and that smile. She wore her hair long, slightly coiffed and unbraided — not the pigtails of 1975. She had on a one-piece, body-fitting outfit — called a *bulaji* in Chinese, but a non-Chinese word derived from Russian *plat'ye* or dress, when the style was imported from the Soviet Union. She was still stunning.

She recognized me too. I rattled off questions: What happened that night? Was she hurt, maltreated, abused? She smiled serenely. She saw I had pushed the button for 12th floor. She pressed the 9th. And as the elevator slowly moved upward, she told me what had happened.

56

"I was very mad and scared that night," she said. "They interrogated me after you left." When the Militia Men established who she was and where she lived, they escorted her home. There, they confirmed that she was the daughter of a patriotic overseas Chinese couple who, in response to Premier Zhou Enlai's invitation, had left the good life and relocated to Beijing to help the Motherland. Thus, she was spared punishment.

I hit the button for the 6th floor to slow down the elevator.

"Then what happened?" I asked.

She endured a tongue-lashing from her parents. The Institute reassigned her father to another college in a nearby district to spare the family further embarrassment. They moved houses and she changed schools. The following summer, Hai Ou graduated from high school and soon after completed a degree in Japanese.

"So how are you now?" I asked hurriedly as the elevator passed the 8th Floor.

Hai Ou said she had just married a foreigner—a Beijing-based Japanese businessman. In fact, she and her husband were temporarily residing in the hotel. She declined to give me their room number, but she held my hand and said she was happy to have known me, and that she'd always remember me, but she had to get on with her life. Sweet, civil, polite but clearly words of a final farewell.

I mumbled something like *wo lijie* (I understand).

She stepped out of the elevator on the 9th floor. She turned around, glanced back at me, and the door shut. I never saw her again.

5

THE GAOKAO

WHAT MADE the Class of '77 different from the politically enthusiastic students I met at Beida back in August 1971? Many, if not most, of those young people so ardently showing off their passion for revolutionary change and spouting the party line against former president Liu Shaoqi would never have qualified for college before the Cultural Revolution. They had been sent to the schools after the government—yes, even the radicals—realized that China needed educated, literate and trained people to run the economy and the bureaucracy. Through the mid-1970s, universities became virtual diploma mills: degrees that once took five years were granted in three, and course content was overwhelmingly focused on revolutionary ideology rather than practical knowledge.

Indeed, Maoist theory demanded that ideological rectitude had to dominate higher education in order to diminish its inherent elitism—the notion that intellectuals were smarter and thus superior to virtuous farmers and laborers. The Chairman decreed that schools should narrow the "three big gaps"—between town and countryside, agriculture and industry, and physical and mental labor. And so the student body had to be made up of the *gong-nong-bing*—in English, workers-peasants-soldiers (WPS).

"Some were educated youths who had spent many years in the countryside, others in factories," explained the historian and Beida professor Wang Xiaoqiu, whose classes I would attend. "They believed political reliability came first and gaining knowledge only second, resulting in their lack of will to study hard."

Learning, Wang said, was a gradual, step-by-step process. Some of the WPS students had received only elementary school education and yet they were blindly enrolled in universities because they had some acceptable revolutionary credentials, such as a poor background. The whole system of learning required a solid foundation of knowledge which the students lacked. Those deficiencies required a complete overhaul of the system after the death of Mao and the end of the Cultural Revolution.

In 1977, Deng Xiaoping had not yet re-emerged as paramount leader, but he was already a force behind the scenes, and he and the other reformers knew that the existing WPS student body of China's universities would not be able to deliver his "Four Modernizations" – in agriculture, industry, science and technology, and defense. So, it was decided, to overhaul the education system. One of the first results was the Class of '77.

This class, the first step towards normalcy after the Cultural Revolution, was selected from a huge number of applicants of the "lost generation," capable students whose studies had been cut short or denied after 1966. The average level of knowledge was much higher than those of the Worker-Peasant-Soldier students, who did not have to pass competitive entrance exams to enroll. The selection process for the Class of '77 was a dramatic throwback to an older China, the revival of competitive qualifying examinations for college admission. It provided an opportunity for those who had been shut out of college for political reasons, but the reputation of the examination's toughness instilled anxiety in all who prepared to take it. A Chinese aphorism aptly describes the National Higher Education Entrance Examination, known in Chinese as *gaokao* – meaning high or top test. The examination was like "tens of thousands of soldiers and horses all squeezing over a bridge made of a single log."

The *gaokao* was administered in November 1977 for the first time since the Red Guards had started terrorizing the country more than a decade before. The label "Class of '77" refers to the year those incoming freshmen took the test, but the students actually started school in the spring of 1978. Loosely speaking, the term "Class of '77" also includes a second batch of Chinese who sat for the exams in the spring of 1978 and enrolled four months after the first examinees. But the historic revival of the *gaokao* in 1977 led to the whole cohort being referred to as the "Class of '77" even though they would only earn their degrees in 1982. All subsequent graduating classes would be tagged with the year they received their diplomas.

The *gaokao* was first instituted in 1952, three years after Mao founded the People's Republic. Although the leaders of the 1949 revolution rejected imperial traditions as being backward and feudal, the *gaokao* obviously evolved out of the ancient system of Civil Service examinations used to recruit the mandarins who for centuries ran the emperor's bureaucracy. That imperial examination process, which required mastery of the Confucian classics, was abolished in 1903. The *gaokao* itself was disrupted just a few years after it began. The first time was in 1958 during the "Great Leap Forward Campaign," a misconceived attempt to catch up with the industrialized West that resulted in severe economic dislocations including tens of millions dead from famine. Then, in the run-up to the Cultural Revolution, the *gaokao* came under intense criticism when the ultra-left wing of the Communist Party attacked it for favoring urbanized, wealthier families who were better situated to enter college than people who lived in farming communities.

The Cultural Revolution resulted not only in the abolition of the *gaokao* in 1966, but also gave free rein to the Red Guard to ransack universities and libraries. All institutes of higher education were closed, and when they were first reopened in 1970, the student body was recruited from the *gong-nong-bing* (WPS). Between then and the revival of the *gaokao* in 1977, about 940,000 WPS students were admitted to college based on recommendations from work and military units and on the basis of ideological correctness. Any attempt at reform was met with ferocious opposition from the radical left.

In 1974, after being rehabilitated for the first time by Zhou Enlai, Deng Xiaoping attempted a gradual reintroduction of the examinations. But Deng was thwarted when the leftists spread the story of Zhang Tiesheng. Zhang was a high school graduate in the northeastern province of Liaoning who during a provincial-level college entrance exam handed in a blank test sheet, with a note on the back saying he had been working eighteen hours a day in a collective farm since 1968, which meant he had no time to study. He argued that the practical results of his farm work were more important than anything he could write on a sheet of paper in an entrance exam. His blank test paper was a protest against what he believed was an examinations monopoly of "truant eggheads." Zhang became a leftist celebrity, lionized by Jiang Qing and hailed as the "blank test paper hero." He was automatically enrolled into the Liaoning Agriculture Institute and inducted into the Communist Party. Deng's attempts at transforming colleges at that point proved to be in vain and he was again purged from the leadership in April 1976.

With the death of Mao and the reversal of fortune for the radicals, however, Deng returned to power. By the time he was formally reinstated into the top leadership in July 1977, he was already actively pushing reforms and initiating new policies. From August 13 to September 25, 1977, the Conference on National University Enrollment in Beijing debated and finally agreed to restore the *gaokao*. "This decision became the impetus for students to study hard and an effective measure to improve the quality of education," read an entry in the official Timeline of the Communist Party, published in 1981 by the People's Publishing House. "It was welcomed by the majority of the people."

In 1977, the Education Department estimated that about twenty million people were qualified to take the exams — meaning, they had managed to graduate from high school during the tumult of the Cultural Revolution. However, because the country's colleges and universities had limited resources, the authorities decided that, in the first year, schools would take in only 230,000 students for four-year undergraduate courses plus 400,000 for technical and vocational courses. In the end, some 5.7 million students were allowed to sit for the three half-day exams conducted nationwide in late November through early December.

Many of the students who were best prepared to take the *gaokao* were the children of "elite intellectuals" (professors, artists and thinkers) and "capitalist roaders" (moderate political opponents of Chairman Mao's dogmatic policies) who had been persecuted during the Cultural Revolution but who never gave up encouraging their children to study. Many of these elite youngsters had been sent to work in the countryside. Even so, they had access to the best educations before the Cultural Revolution and they were aware of the kind of facts, figures, and traditional and political literature they needed to know by heart — if not memorized — to pass the national college entrance exam. After years of hard labor, they were also the ones most eager to resume their studies. It was suddenly a chance to escape what seemed to be their doom of relegation to a life of agricultural and rural servitude.

There was still substantial ideological concern about the pedigree of the new students, even after they passed the *gaokao*. In Beida's journalism department, some officials wanted to defer applications by individuals whose records indicated, for example, that their "grandparents are in Taiwan," or "father is a Rightist," or "family's 'Cultural Revolution' problem remains unresolved." But Zhang Longxiang, the university's vice chancellor in charge of enrollment, declared that such background problems should not influence normal enrollment.

The subjects tested by the *gaokao* included Chinese language and literature, math, history, geography, and politics. As I know from experience, if you don't read and write Chinese constantly, you forget the characters and the phrases. A basic knowledge of the language requires knowledge of 1,500 characters, and how they combine to create a myriad technical and colloquial terms and expressions. To pass the *gaokao*, you probably had to know at least 3,000 characters. That was hard enough for urban students. In the rural communes where many young people were exiled, it was much more difficult. There just weren't enough books for one to read and practice.

For those who hoped to study humanities, the *gaokao* also had a section that tested mastery of foreign languages. There, the test of translating Chinese into English was still decidedly ideological. My schoolmate Tang Wenfang, who taught himself English (in part by reading a surreptitiously passed on pirated copy of Masters and Johnson's *Human Sexual Response*) while working for a chemical factory, can still remember the stiltedness of the long passage he had to interpret—and his helplessness at not knowing the English equivalents of the Chinese propaganda terms. "I am a new member of the Red Star Commune," the exam text began. "Two years ago, I left the city and settled down in the countryside. The party is now calling on young people to study science and technology in order to achieve the great goals of the Four Modernizations. I am taking the college entrance examination now. I hope I will be accepted. I pledge that I will study hard for the revolution and become red and expert. If I am not accepted, I will return to the countryside and work equally hard for the revolution. I will contribute to the construction of our motherland as a great and modern socialist country."

There was much ambivalence among some test-takers and their families.

"My mother was suspicious of the new changes," said my classmate Bai Weiji, who was working at a car manufacturing plant when the *gaokao* was announced. She didn't want him to go to college. "After seeing so many bad things that happened to intellectuals during the Cultural Revolution, my mother said that it was better for me to remain a factory worker all my life."

Tang Wenfang had the opposite experience. He wasn't keen on taking the exams when they were announced. At twenty-two, he enjoyed his "iron rice bowl" — that big pot of social benefits that the Communist regime doled out to good worker-citizens at state-owned factories. Wenfang had a stable job at a chemical plant, a regular income, subsidized board and lodging, and medical care. But his mother thought the *gaokao* was his last chance to get a college education. After some hectoring, she got her way.

But most young people who took the *gaokao* at the end of 1977 probably shared the feelings and expectations, if not the experience, of my friend and former history classmate, Chen Yanni. She had virtually resigned herself to a dismal life in the countryside or doing menial work in the city. When the Cultural Revolution broke out, her family was on the wrong side of the political divide. Yanni's father, a journalist and a senior editor at Xinhua News Agency, was accused of being a "capitalist roader" and sent to various labor camps. Her elder brother and sister were ordered to work in the countryside even before they could finish high school. Yanni was lucky enough to have finished high school before she was assigned to a commune in Daxing County, just south of Beijing. After a year or so there, she felt her life was at a dead end. "The times were bleak," she told me. "I thought that after leaving the village, I could go to the city and work as a janitor or a street sweeper. Those were the types of jobs for children of officials like my parents who got into political trouble."

She had been in Daxing for two years when, in November 1977, she heard that the college entrance exams were to be held the next month. It was a chance to escape what she thought was her fate, but could she take enough time off from work in the commune to prepare for the test?

Fortunately, Zhang Hecai, the village leader of Daxing, had also finished high school and valued education. "He told me that *gaokao* was back and if any of the 'rusticated youths' in our unit wished to take it, we could go home and prepare," Yanni recalled. There was opposition. Most of the peasants said that letting the young people take days off would reduce farm productivity but Zhang overruled them.

Having the time to study was one thing, but what would Yanni study? Apart from tracts of propaganda and the exemplary lives of revolutionaries, books were hard to find. "Most of the books and audio records in our home were ransacked, burned or taken away by the Red Guards during the Cultural Revolution," she said. "It was hard to find good books." She remembers her parents used to keep a copy of *Jin Ping Mei*, a 17th century erotic novel and a masterpiece of Chinese literature. But when the Cultural Revolution started, her mother shredded the book and flushed it down the toilet. There were certainly no schools in the area that offered revision courses, not even groups of potential test-takers forming study groups. "I met up a few times with my older sister, who had also planned to take the *gaokao*," she recalled. "We did not know what questions to expect so we simply re-read our high school textbooks and drilled each other with questions and answers."

A few of her trusted friends passed around Chinese editions of foreign classics but Yanni realized that Tolstoy's *Anna Karenina*, Stendahl's *The Red and the Black*, and Pushkin's poems were banned as "poisonous weeds" during the Cultural Revolution. She said she did not really want to read the "bad books" but desperately needed material to practice reading Chinese characters. So she read them in secret.

On the day of the *gaokao*, the village leader arranged for a tractor to take Yanni and three other youngsters from the village to the exam site about six kilometers away. They found themselves among hundreds of other nervous young people. Yanni said that most of the *gaokao* questions were "fill-in-the-blanks" that required having memorized lots of dates and numbers by rote.

"There were questions like 'When did the Opium War break out?' or 'What treaties were imposed on China after it lost the Opium War'?" Other questions required examinees to write a sentence using specific Chinese characters. A large part of the test, worth about twenty percent, required examinees to write an essay.

"I recall the topic was something like—'Me, in this Year of Struggle'," said Yanni, adding that she did not have to struggle too hard to write the essay. She had kept up her writing during the bad years.

Waiting for the exam results, however, "seemed like an eternity." Every examinee had to list three schools they wanted to enter in order of preference; Yanni's first choice was Peking University. But as she waited, she heard rumors that Beida had already sent out acceptance letters. Why hadn't she received hers? "I was quite disappointed thinking I did not get in," she said. "I went back to my village and decided to just prepare for the next *gaokao*."

A few weeks later, however, Yanni was told to go to the office of the village chief. "The man sorting letters rifled through a bunch of envelopes and handed me one with my name on it," she said. "The envelope had a Beida logo and my heart jumped in anticipation. I opened the envelope and read the letter that said I had been accepted to Beida. I did not cry, I just literally dropped to the floor and sat there for a good ten minutes. I read and re-read the acceptance letter. I could not believe it."

Her life — like hundreds of thousands who were accepted into college in 1977 — was about to change. "Passing the *gaokao* and getting accepted at Beida gave me a second chance."

Yanni and I became friends and classmates. We both appreciated a story that occurred eleven years after we enrolled — an example of history as payback. In July 1988, Mao Xinyu, the late Chairman Mao's grandson, graduated from Peking University-affiliated High School. He took the *gaokao* but, as the story goes, his scores were not good enough. His mother Shao Hua, who was a Beida graduate, contacted Beida's chancellor, Ding Shisun.

"For three generations our family have belonged to Beida," she reportedly told Ding as she tried to argue for her son's admission into the most prestigious school in China. But Ding said admission "does not necessarily follow" upon a family's history of education and privilege. According to the story, Shao insisted that "Xinyu should go to Beida." The chancellor remained steadfast, saying, "Beida has a free spirit, students are active, I'm afraid we will be unable to ensure his safety if he enrolls here." With that, Mao's grandson enrolled in another university.

6

ORIGINS

IN THE YEARS in the countryside leading up to my acceptance into Beida in 1977, I suffered deep and constant longings to see my Amang and Inang—my Dad and Mom—and feel and taste the life in the barrio outside Manila where I grew up. In the little village of Liang, in Bulacan province, everyone, every family, knew each other. Home, as I envisioned it in my exile, was carefree and idyllic: playing hide-and-seek with the neighbor kids; competing to make the best tops, kites, and slingshots; learning to swim in the river behind our house. On rainy days when school was out, we roamed the town, combing through trees and bushes in search of a special type of fighting spider which we'd collect in matchboxes, and ready to pit against each other in arachnid sparring sessions.

Liang was a barrio of Malolos, the provincial capital, which was an hour's drive north of Manila. Today, the sprawl of the metropolis has reached it, but back then it was a world apart. We were very proud of Malolos and its historic role in the uprising against the Spanish, who ruled the islands for more than 300 years. The Philippines' first constitution was drafted here by the Malolos Congress, which on June 4, 1898 declared the archipelago's independence from the Spaniards, making the islands the first republic in Asia. But the event turned out to be an episode in a historic drama that was both tragedy and farce. Filipinos had risen against Spain, but the fading European power had also just lost a war against the rising United States of America. (Admiral George Dewey and his ships wiped out the Spanish fleet docked in Manila Bay in a six-hour battle on May 1, 1898). The Treaty of Paris signed on December 10, 1898 between the two countries turned the Philippines over to the Americans—ignoring the Philippine declaration of independence. U.S. troops soon swept in to put down what they called the Philippine insurrection—leading to the death of as many as 200,000 Filipinos. The resulting U.S.-governed territory in Southeast Asia was a cultural mishmash: an overwhelmingly Roman Catholic populace with Spanish surnames and, because of an effective U.S. educational system, mostly fluent in English.

My surname is Spanish, composed of the word for flower and the one for cross; but no one has any idea of its origins. My Amang—Dad—was named Cenon, born to a family of modest means. His parents taught their children the value of hard work and education. He had a good role model in his father, Felix, a slightly built, charismatic man who in his prime led a detachment of Katipuneros, the revolutionary group who fought the Spanish colonial army in the late 1890s.

Grandfather Felix's strong suit was education. He finished high school at the Colegio de San Juan de Letran in Manila and was fluent in Spanish and Filipino. He wrote beautiful calligraphy. After the anti-Spain revolution, he did clerical work for the town government. He was also active in local politics—he was elected city councilor—and was instrumental in setting up a new elementary school in his barrio. He was only in his 40s when he died of illness.

The sole responsibility of rearing the six FlorCruz children fell on the shoulders of my widowed grandmother, Rosenda. She worked hard. She made dresses and sold them in public markets. She took in boarders. Whatever she saved, she invested in the education of all her children. Her two elder daughters, Rufina and Illuminada, still in their late teens at that time, went on to complete teaching certificates after high school. They quickly found teaching jobs and helped pay for the education of their four younger brothers through high school.

In the end, all six children acquired a college education. In 1952, a Philippine magazine, *Weekly Women's Magazine*, honored my grandmother and her brood as "Family of the Year," citing the family as a "fine example of family cooperation in the face of odds."

My paternal grandparents died before I was born. But I do have fond memories of my maternal grandfather, Trifon Adriano. Tall and well built, he was known to be a good baseball player in his prime. He loved politics as an avocation. He was well-read, full of dry humor and wit.

He was a civil servant all his life and retired as Bulacan's provincial treasurer. His wife, my grandmother Rosario, was a homemaker but she and my grandfather managed to send all their children through college. He and his family lived in a house just across the street from ours. We often shared meals together, in our home or his. When I woke up in the morning, I would see him sitting by the window reading the daily newspapers. I sometimes walked over to his house to read newspapers with him or chat about current events.

My Amang, Cenon, was a perennial valedictorian and topnotcher in school. He became a lawyer and a chemist, which helped him get a job as a sugar technologist for the government – a key position overseeing the quality of the Philippines' major export. He rose up the government bureaucracy and retired as the Deputy General Manager of the Philippine Sugar Institute, the country's top think tank and supervisory body of the sugar industry. On the year he retired in the early 1980s, he was given a Presidential Award as "Civil Servant of the Year."

My Inang, Lourdes, was a college graduate, which was not ordinary during her time. Like Amang, she attended the University of the Philippines — which had been set up by the Americans and would gain the reputation as the best school in the country. After a brief stint as a high school teacher in our hometown, she used her Home Economics degree to build a career at the Department of Agriculture. From the 1950s through the '80s, she led a job-training team that helped impoverished women in the Bulacan province earn extra income for their families by learning horticulture, cooking and handicrafts. She kept a busy schedule, doing her government job and engaging in social and community activities while rearing us six children.

I was born on April 5, 1951, the fifth of six children and baptized Jaime Vicente FlorCruz. The date was the feast day of St. Vincent Ferrer, hence my middle name. As for my first name Jaime, my parents thought I should be named after a handsome Filipino movie actor named Jaime Dela Rosa.

I had a miserable childhood. Just one week after birth, my parents recalled, rashes broke out on my face and later all over my body. I was in constant pain and irritable. My parents applied all sorts of skin ointments and took me to every known specialist, even to the *arbolaryo* (folk doctors who prescribed traditional herbs and practiced faith healing) — all to no avail. Many days, they said, I was wrapped in cheesecloth sheets to keep me from scratching and to ease the persistent itch on my neck, arms, legs and virtually all parts of my body, including my scalp. "Only Jaime's eyeballs were spared from the universal eczema," my father wrote in his memoir. Years later, my mother described to me how forlorn and frustrated she was about my condition.

"You were in constant pain, scratching and moaning, that once I pleaded to God to please take you if you will be in such pain for long."

My misery eased years later when my father got hold of a prescription by a certain Dr. Fischer which was known to have cured the eczema of a relative's friend. It did not come easy. My father had to scour the town to get the perfect ointment because most drug stores did not have all the ingredients listed in the prescription. Finally, one pharmacist whom my father had met years earlier was able to fill the prescription. Seven years of painful itching finally ended. Seven years! This miserable childhood must have conditioned me to have a high threshold for pain, to be patient and resilient.

But my misery pales compared to what my parents and elder siblings endured during World War II.

Nieva, the eldest sister, was barely one year old and my mother was expecting a second child when the Japanese invaded the Philippines. Soon, the Japanese army closed in on our hometown, Malolos, a strategic location close to Clark Airfield. Japanese military planes periodically strafed the provincial capitol building, just two kilometers from our house. Each time planes appeared, my mother, along with her parents, siblings and infant Nieva, would scurry into an air-raid shelter dug at a corner of the backyard. They could hear rumblings of warplanes and convoys of trucks crisscrossing our hometown day and night.

All this time, my mother had to care for her two daughters without my father, who months earlier had left home to join the Philippine Army in a far-flung region to fight the Japanese invasion. Her savings depleted, she had to depend on her parents' support to buy milk and other essential goods. They traded rice and firewood to cover household expenses. Irma, the second child, was born on February 14, 1942, at the height of the Japanese occupation. Then tragedy struck. One week after birth, mother started bleeding. Lonely and worried about my father's fate, she became delirious. The left side of her body, her arm and leg, got paralyzed. She could not open her eyes, move her lips or swallow anything, not even drops of water.

Fear constantly plagued her and my siblings. In early April, a Japanese garrison moved in to Malolos. They put the town under curfew and soldiers patrolled the streets day and night. One night, my mother recalled, a Japanese patrol saw a light in the house, went in and walked straight up to the room where my mother was lying sick in bed. "Why was there a lighted lamp?" the soldier yelled, lifting the mosquito net with his saber, pointing its tip to my mother. Petrified, her parents who stood next to the bed, explained that Inang was very ill. The soldier left.

In the middle of April, two months after she became half-paralyzed, Inang started to feel a creeping sensation on her left side, thanks to the daily massage and spiritual healing done by a town *espiritista*, a faith healer. Weeks later, she was able to sit on the bed by herself. Another week later, she could stand by holding onto a chair. That was my mother's physical condition when my father, after evading Japanese checkpoints, sneaked back home on May 29, 1942. "I personally attended to the needs of Luding (my mother's nickname) and the children, held them, played with them, and took them out for walks and snacks, all of which were missed during my absence of six months," my father later recalled.

The post-war years were bountiful. During that time, my brothers Rene and Nilo were born before me, and my sister Leni was born two years after me, rounding out our family to three girls and three boys.

We were a double-income family, and in 1950 my parents

were able to build a new house with several rooms and a big yard. We were one of the first households in our hometown to own a car and a television. But my parents kept us grounded. Amang was a stern disciplinarian. He expected his children to do well in school and at home. He encouraged us to visit and play with friends and neighbors, but he expected us to be back home before the church bells rang for the Angelus prayer at 6 p.m. when Catholic tradition dictated that families gather at home to pray.

I remember a few times dashing home with my youngest sister Leni, just minutes late for prayer. For this minor infraction, we got a tongue-lashing. But there were days when we kept on playing in the neighborhood, forgot the time and arrived quite late. That called for a thrashing. Amang told us to lie prone on the floor and he whipped us with his leather belt. He restrained his swing but it still hurt when it landed. Years later, Leni and I learned that before my elder brother Nilo received his punishment for the same infraction, he managed to pad his butt with a magazine.

My parents expected us to help in housework, even though we employed house helpers. On typical weekends, Amang gave us duties, written up as bullet points on a green board. For the three boys, the Sunday list included chores like "dig holes and plant coconut seedlings" or "prune the trees," "wash the car," or "rotate the tires." My sisters helped Inang cook our meals and tended to the plants and orchids.

I have beautiful memories of my childhood in Malolos. In our neighborhood, virtually everyone, every family, knew each other. I played hide-and-seek with neighbors. On the street we played *piko*, a Filipino version of hopscotch, and, *tumbang preso*, or jailbreak, that involved players knocking down an empty can with slippers followed by a chase. My playmates came from various social strata. Among my best friends were my two next-door neighbors, whose parents ran a *carinderia* — a porridge-and-snack stand — in the town's public market. We all took pride in being born and bred in Malolos, a historic town, now a city, which is known as home to many nationalist heroes, writers, poets, and women's rights advocates.

My parents provided the family with a comfortable life. More important, they surrounded us with books, newspapers, and magazines. They were voracious readers. For years, ever since my childhood, my father subscribed to various newspapers and magazines. He often browsed bookstores on home ground and overseas, and he brought home books that he always stamped "Ex Libris... FlorCruz Library."

They whetted our curiosity about other cultures through their frequent travels. Whenever they returned from overseas trips, they brought home souvenirs — cheese from Denmark, a shepherd's horn from Switzerland, or a vinyl record of The Beatles from London. Each time my mother came back from travels, she whipped up a new foreign dish that she had just learned. After each overseas trip, my father would set up our projector and gather us all in the home "library" to show the color slides he took of his travels.

My parents taught us to think "international" and "global," even before these became fashionable buzzwords. Because of their extensive travels and multifaceted social and professional activities, they had a network of friends from all over the world. Many times, we hosted their visits and homestays.

They also taught us to be hospitable and inclusive. Although they personally suffered hardships and trauma at the hands of Japanese military invaders during World War II, they kept an open mind toward the Japanese people. In the early 1980s, our family hosted Masako Gomi, an exchange scholar from Japan, who stayed in our house for a year.

I grew up a gregarious, self-confident boy. When I was around seven, I joined a talent contest during a Christmas party hosted by the Jaycees Club (my father was an active member.) I sang *Teddy Bear* a la Elvis Presley and won a prize.

Like my other siblings, I attended Immaculata Academy, a private Catholic school, until I reached Grade 5, when my parents moved me and my younger sister Leni to Central Elementary School, a public school. My parents, it turned out, were turned off by the Catholic nuns at the elementary school because they were pressuring my elder brother Rene, who had just finished elementary grades, to go to a seminary and become a priest, a vocation he did not want. He instead enrolled in a public high school and later became a medical doctor.

The abrupt move forced me to adapt to a new school system and to make new friends. I did quite well in class but was never an academic standout, except in one writing contest, in which my essay won first prize.

Graduating in a public elementary school made it easier to move into a public high school not far from home, where my two elder brothers went. Before enrollment, I took a placement examination that got me into Section 1, one of the two "pilot classes" of our cohort based on our entrance exam grades. The sizes of the two sections were kept to about two dozen students each. We were taught math, physics and chemistry courses that were more advanced than the norm.

I was not on top of the class academically but I was active in extracurricular activities and quite popular on campus. I was an active member of the Boy Scouts and the student newspaper. I joined school plays and public debate. I ran and won as a representative in the student government. I represented the school in a city-wide oratorical contest and took home the bronze medal.

While I was partial to writing and had the gift of gab, I did not have a clear career goal then. Growing up as a teenager in the Philippines, I had naïve personal ambitions, like most middle-class kids of my generation. Even though I was educated in Philippine culture and history, and I was good at these, I was also steeped in American culture, thanks to all the books and publications I read and all the TV programs I watched. At home, I binge-watched cartoons like Popeye, war flicks like Combat and classics like Tarzan, Zorro and Gulliver's Travels. I was also fond of Hollywood movies and Broadway musicals.

At a tender age, I bought into the American Dream. When I was around ten, I was so obsessed with the TV cartoon *Dick Tracy* that I even convinced my mother to give me money so that I could order by mail a set of toys — a plastic wristwatch that doubled as a walkie-talkie, plus a tin badge as a member of the U.S.-based Dick Tracy Club. When I was a senior in high school, I was keen to apply for an American Field Service (AFS) Scholarship, which offered a chance of a homestay while studying in a U.S. high school. It turned out that applicants had to be seventeen years old by the start of the school year, so I did not qualify.

Like my parents, my four elder siblings went to the University of the Philippines. I didn't. When I graduated from high school, I wasn't quite at the top of the class academically. I wasn't particularly ambitious either. I simply wished to finish college, find a steady job, marry a beautiful girl and perhaps drive a red Mustang. Still, I did well enough in an entrance exam to be accepted into the Jesuit-run all-boys Ateneo de Manila University. It was one of best in the Philippines, and the most expensive. It attracted the sons of rich and well-connected families, some of whom drove to school in red Mustangs.

A degree from the Ateneo put you on a fast track to success.

There was also a distinctive Ateneo accent—polished, more American, without the broad vowels and hard consonants of regional Filipino dialects. Many graduates of the Ateneo became top politicians, corporate lawyers, bankers, and captains of industry. But I was totally out of place. I felt like a *provinciano*, or country hick.

Most of my schoolmates were city-bred and had known each other since childhood. When I got to the school, there were already well-formed cliques. To make friends and try to fit in, I joined the college paper as a cub reporter. I auditioned and joined the college glee club and we rehearsed almost daily. I placed first in a school-wide Sunday run and was promptly recruited into the varsity track team.We practiced three afternoons a week. I joined parties and soirees with girls from neighboring Catholic colleges, Maryknoll and St. Theresa's—the all-girl equivalents of Ateneo. My social life soared, but I struggled with academics. I flunked Math and English and was kicked out after a year.

Shamed and devastated, I felt I'd let down my family, which had a two-generation run of putting its kids through top-rate universities. I became the black sheep of the family. My parents were disappointed, but they refrained from browbeating me. "Pick yourself up where you stumbled," my father counseled. In 1968, my father decided to enroll me at the Philippine College of Commerce (PCC), one of Manila's poor man's colleges better known for producing office secretaries and accountants rather than lawyers and doctors.

But the year I got to PCC—1968—was one of upheaval around the world. The U.S. war in Vietnam was raging. China was in the middle of its chaotic Cultural Revolution. From San Francisco to Paris, from Munich to Manila, students were raging against American imperialism and setting up protest barricades on campus. The PCC, the nondescript college my father had picked for his ne'er-do-well son, quickly became an epicenter of student activism in Manila. And I joined the frontlines of the protest, learning the taste of police tear gas from behind the barricades.

I became the editor-in-chief of *Ang Malaya* (The Free), our college paper, a lead actor in the school's protest theater and the president of a national editors' league. These were my pulpits as a grimly determined advocate for social and political change. My theater group performed on stage, on the picket lines and during street demonstrations. We demanded academic freedom. We called for a free and democratic society. We denounced social inequality and warned the public of the looming military dictatorship of Ferdinand Marcos—who had been elected in 1966 and was nearing the end of his first presidential term. In 1070, he resorted to "goons, guns and gold" to get reelected for another four-year term—leading to inflation and unemployment. With growing public discontent, we stepped up street protests. Supporters called us catalysts of change. Critics labeled us troublemakers, communist agitators and "pinkos."

One day, at the end of a mass protest, I and a small group of demonstrators were accosted by a team of armed police officers. They pinned us down on the pavement, face down, and started to kick us. My chin hit the pavement and started bleeding. When I turned over to protest, a police officer hit me on my head with his rifle butt. I sustained a deep cut and blacked out. When I regained consciousness, I found myself in a police station. I spent the night in a city jail for allegedly "resisting arrest" and "possessing deadly weapons"—all trumped-up charges. They had planted a knife in my jacket pocket when I was unconscious. I spent the night in jail and was released on bail. Still, I was formally charged in a city court.

For one week, I nursed my wounds at home. My father sternly advised: stay home and keep a low profile. Refrain from joining mass protests. I had only rare discussions on politics with my parents. While we agreed on the problems with the Marcos government—corruption, bureaucracy, social inequality—and conceded the need for reforms, we disagreed on solutions. While they understood why we took to the streets, they worried most about my personal safety. "We fear that one day, you will disappear and we won't know where to pick up your body," my father told me.

Still, my fellow activists and I remained fearless. On March 20, 1970, soon after I was beaten up and arrested by police, my then girlfriend mailed me a get-well card, with a hand-written note.

"I've been getting reports about your being caught and being hurt during the anti-poverty march last Tuesday," she wrote. "It didn't come to me much of a surprise though because with what I know about your commitment, you're ready to sacrifice everything, not sparing your life for the sake of 'your nationalism'. Nevertheless, I worry myself to death thinking of how you are and what will happen to you after that unforgettable experience... I want to hear your voice so badly—to give me peace.... Remember when you asked me what would I feel if you die in one of these demonstrations? I didn't feel so sure of myself then, but now I'm quite sure of the answer. Don't you ever ask that question again—forever.... I miss you very much. Wish I were there to take care of you."

Personal safety was no longer in my mind. Police brutality changed the trajectory of my life. I had lost trust in our political system and I was seething with anger. Before that episode, the slogans "Down with Fascism!" and "Down with the Marcos Dictatorship!" seemed like mere slogans. After that, the slogans became real. Instead of getting scared, I was outraged. Instead of quitting, I was fired up.

In 1970, a police team raided our PCC campus. They accused our school of being a hub of anti-government protesters and dissidents. They arrested several students and school staff and were also looking for the editor of the radical school paper — me. Fortunately, the police came at night and I was at home in Malolos.

The repression would continue as part of the orchestrated brutality against a "communist conspiracy" that Marcos would cite as the rationale for putting the entire country under martial law in September 1972.

Before Marcos began what would turn out to be nearly a dozen years of autocratic rule, a bombing incident rocked the Philippine capital and changed my life abruptly. The night of August 21, 1971 — our first day in China — grenades were thrown onto a stage in Manila where politicians opposing Marcos were holding a political rally. Six people died and scores were wounded, including prominent leaders opposing President Marcos. Hours later, Marcos ordered the police to round up hundreds of his political opponents and critics. Many were jailed indefinitely. Those who went into hiding were put on black-list.

To this day, there are two conflicting explanations of what happened, who orchestrated the bombing and why. One claims that the government staged the attack to build up its case for the imposition of martial law the next year, akin to Hitler burning the Reichstag and blaming it on his opponents. The other alleges that local communist cadres pulled off the bloody incident to exacerbate the political conflicts, provoke government repression and create a revolutionary situation.

We wouldn't hear of the tumult in Manila till later. At the time, we were on a train steaming through southern China and then a plane to Beijing. I was completely enamored by the idea of China.

Like my compatriots, I was curious to see what was going on in China, which boasted that it was building a new socialist China under the leadership of the "great, glorious and correct" Communist Party. I could barely understand the gobbledygook slogans and unfamiliar ideas, but I was keen to discern the whys and wherefores and perhaps learn lessons from the China experience. Little did I know that the three-week tour would turn into an open-ended life of exile and experiences in a giant nation, through the chaos of the Cultural Revolution and on into the dynamic years that have followed.

I did romanticize China. I imagined a socialist utopia, where people lived simple but stable lives, where the state provided cradle-to-grave jobs, as well as all essential goods and public services such as healthcare, housing and education. In this ideal place, everyone would "serve the people" and work for the collective good. And because there was no disparity between the rich and the poor, and everyone was treated equally, there would be no corruption, no crime and no social unrest. Even after the first few weeks of visiting factories, people's communes, hospitals and schools, I thought all these musings were true. There were no flies. And there were no policemen with guns.

In fact, it turned out that China in 1971 was still in the middle of an upheaval. Radical-minded ideologues, including Chairman Mao's closest advisers and his wife Jiang Qing, opposed efforts to open up and modernize China. They attacked Communist Party leaders like Deng Xiaoping who advocated results-driven reforms. "It does not matter if it's a black cat or a white cat," Deng famously remarked. "As long as it catches mice, it's a good cat." Mao loyalists condemned such pragmatism as "revisionist" heresy. For the third time in his political career, Deng was forced out of office for pursuing his vision of a prosperous, open-door China, albeit one still firmly ruled by the Communist Party.

I had no idea of just how turbulent the times were beneath the surface. When we first arrived in Beijing, Lin Biao, the defense minister and Mao's anointed successor, was the toast of the state media, hailed in the newspapers, radio and television as a brilliant military strategist and a loyal Mao follower. His pictures were all over town, all over the country, second only to Mao's in prominence. Among his many achievements, he was credited with having masterminded the creation of Mao's "little red book." But a month after we arrived, Lin was gone. The story gradually trickled in, unofficially: Lin had been killed in a plane crash, perhaps shot down, while fleeing towards the Soviet Union. He was accused of staging a failed coup. We were totally oblivious that Lin Biao had become the villain, until my friends and I noticed that we were the only ones still toting Mao's little red book and wearing the ubiquitous Mao pins. Even our Chinese hosts had stopped the cult-like idolatry. What's going on? Where to, China?

For years until Mao's death and the end of the Cultural Revolution in 1976, political brinkmanship between the Maoist and reformist factions raged inside the Communist Party structure. The economy remained weak and fragile. Ordinary citizens normally declined to discuss politics with us in any way, but when we did have conversations with them, they seemed disheartened, demoralized and cynical. Driven by ideology and political correctness, and fearful of losing control, the Communist Party determined every aspect of the lives of ordinary people, what they could and could not do: where to work, where to live, whom to marry, and how many children to have. It decided for citizens which school to attend, what career to pursue, what books to read and what movies to watch. Ordinary people had no choices.

This was the New China that I stumbled into. This was the

adopted home to which I had to adapt.

The news from Manila finally reached us. The August 21 bombing of the political rally was shocking enough. But Marcos had also suspended the writ of habeas corpus, allowing the authorities to make summary arrests of anyone, without a need for a warrant. Out of our group, Chito Sta Romana, Eric Baculinao, Grace Punongbayan, Rey Tiquia, and myself were likely to be arrested upon arrival home. I was worried about the knife the police had planted into my pocket in that arrest and the standing court case against me. The other four were among the several activists formally charged with subversion, the news splashed all over the local papers.

And so we decided to stay indefinitely. Weeks turned to months, months to years. The waiting turned out to be fruitless. Four years into our forced exile, there were no signs that the Philippine government was easing up on its "enemies" to allow us to get back home.

"We are much younger than Marcos," we told ourselves, "We can outlive him."

And we did.

But first we had to live in China.

7

COMMUNIST PARTY ANIMALS

THE PROSPECT of sitting for the *gaokao* terrified me. My grasp of written and spoken Chinese was infinitely better than when I was first sent to the countryside, but the nuances of political Chinese — and the correct phraseology to express those nuances — were still not instinctive. The idea that I would have to prove it under pressure of an exam caused me much anxiety.

To my immense relief, there was an advantage to being a foreigner — which I discovered with a simple phone call to Beida's foreign students' office. "We accept the academic credits you earned in the Philippines and in the Beijing Languages Institute," the office functionary assured me. All I had to do to gain admittance to Beida was pass a placement exam: a simple reading and writing test to check my proficiency in intermediate Chinese.

It took all of thirty minutes compared to the two half-day sessions of the *gaokao*. Beida's Class of '77 would include about 160 foreign students, mostly from North Vietnam, Laos, Albania, and North Korea — Communist allies of the People's Republic. There were students from the Third World, mostly from Africa and the Middle East, but the university would also have students from Japan, Canada, France, Italy, Britain, the Netherlands, Denmark, Iceland, and other Western countries. I was the only one from the Philippines. Most enrolled for only one year on scholarship as exchange students, or on junior-year-abroad programs. Less than half took the full, four-year course, as I did.

Despite the presence of students from outside China, I found it just as easy to fit in with my Chinese schoolmates. For one, I could now converse fluently with them in Mandarin; also, as a Southeast Asian, I could pass for Chinese. I wore what everyone else did at the time: baggy pants, a Mao jacket and cap, and black canvas slip-on shoes. I had added a few revolutionary and folk songs to my repertoire, like "I Stand Guard as a Sentry for the Motherland," a People's Liberation Army soldier's ballad, and "A Never-Setting Sun Rises on the Grassland," an old Mongolian tune that had been transformed into a paean to Mao. And of course, I belted out arias from "Taking Tiger Mountain By Stratagem" that Teacher Song had taught me down on the farm in Xiangjiang.

Like my Chinese friends, I had been subjected to incessant indoctrination through the media and popular culture, so I was familiar with Maoist mythology—and the political correctness of admiring proletarian saints like Lei Feng, the foot soldier and paragon of Communist selflessness. The textbooks I used at the Beijing Language Institute repeated tales of the soldier-saint Lei Feng helping old women crossing streets, and of doing his comrades' laundry in secret, somehow mysteriously captured in photographs. His motto was supposed to be a universal truth held by all: "To be a small screw in the machine serving the Communist Party, Chairman Mao and the people." That was reflected in a ballad with lyrics lifted from his diary: "Parents are dear to their children, but they can't compare with Chairman Mao." I could sing that one too. Tragically, Lei Feng died when a telephone pole fell on his head.

Myths and music were entertaining, but the main reason I

gravitated toward my Chinese classmates was our history of shared suffering. I too had been sent away to learn from the laboring classes, as Mao had decreed. Though my time on the farm and in trawler boats in no way compared with their hardships, it gave us common ground. We all hoped for an end to the mindless radical campaigns based on Maoist dogma, all of which had brought chaos, stagnation and tragedy. We knew what did not work. We all wished for change. In the Chinese language, there is a way of saying "we" — *zanmen* — that indicates that everyone in the conversation belongs to the same group, an inclusive and intimate "we." When my friends talked to me, they often slipped into saying *"zanmen Zhongguo ren"* — "we Chinese" — which included me. I found it flattering whenever they mistook me for Chinese, or at least forgot that I was a foreigner.

I was assigned a bed in Building 26, a three-story men's dormitory just inside the south gate of the Beida compound. Home to about a hundred students, mostly foreigners, it was in a convenient spot. Not far from the gate were a bus stop, a bank, a grocery, and the state-owned Long March Restaurant, which served draft beer and a limited menu of sauteed dishes. In addition to the heavily subsidized and thus very cheap, simple meals at the cafeteria, all these establishments were conveniently located so I could spend the stipends the government provided me and all students with to buy food, toiletries, and other necessities.

Beida charged nothing for tuition. But that meant the school had little budget for spending on student accommodations. My room — which I shared with one other person — was spartan, with just enough space for two beds, two desks, two chairs and a closet. I avoided leaning on the walls because the powdery white paint stuck to my clothes. I was issued a pillow and bedding, an enamel basin, a towel and a thermos flask. The last item was a necessity. I needed it to store drinking water because nothing that flowed out of Beijing's taps was potable. To get the hot water for both drinking and washing, I had to walk to a boiler room behind the dorm. In winter, the trip there and back was dreadful because temperatures often dove well below freezing. Even when the weather was cold, heating in the dorms was limited. It was turned on in the early morning and evening and turned off during daytime.

The facilities—bathrooms and toilets—were communal as well as cold, drafty and dimly-lit. Only squat toilets were provided, but at least they were separated into stalls and had locking doors, a great improvement over the outdoor latrines I had had to use in the Hunan farm. The showers had no partitions, with hot water available only from five o'clock to seven in the evening. That schedule overlapped with dinnertime and posed a real dilemma for all of us. "Wash and starve, or eat and smell," quipped a British dorm mate.

The students did their laundry during the weekends and in their spare time. There were, of course, no washing machines in the dark, unheated room set aside for the chore. We hand-washed our clothes in the Beida-provided enamel basins, using "White Cat"-brand laundry detergent and cold water.

Like the rest of the dorms, there was only one telephone in Building 26. It sat in the doorkeeper's room on the ground floor. Each time there was an incoming call, Old Man Zhang, the portly guard, would step out and yell the room number and name of the person who had received the call. Residents on the upper floors could barely hear him.

While the living conditions of foreign students weren't luxurious, Chinese students fared worse. They normally lived in fifteen square-meter rooms with four sets of bunk beds, accommodating six to eight people. Foreign students had ten square-meter rooms shared by two people. Overseas students also had more access to hot water and heating, grain, cotton and cooking oil.

"Food for foreign students was better than those for the Chinese because meat supplies for Chinese nationals was limited and rationed," recalled Wang Wenquan, an officer at the Foreign Students' Office, in one of our casual chats a few years after I graduated. "Besides, the foreign students were considered our honored guests."

Chinese students went around with their own bowls and chopsticks in their bags because the cafeterias did not provide ample utensils. The lunchrooms often didn't have enough benches so many students ate while standing around tables. Some did not bother to eat inside the cafeterias at all, buying bowls of congee (gruel) and *mantou* (steamed buns) from the cafeterias before heading straight back to the classroom or library.

Foreign and local students were not supposed to mingle too closely. While my language skills and appearance allowed me to get closer to the Chinese students, foreign students were discouraged from socializing with them in shops, theaters, buses and trains and in friends' homes. We suspected that this was done to prevent fraternization, although officials claimed it was to maintain our "safety and security." Whenever we protested about this segregation, our Chinese handlers said, half-jokingly, "There are still class enemies around."

Unlike most foreign students, I signed up for the four-year undergraduate degree in Chinese history. I chose to major in contemporary history, because, as a left-leaning Filipino activist, I was most interested in what happened right before and after the Communist Party took over China in 1949. But historical truth was hard to come by, and the search for it a challenge. History turned out to be a battleground where the country's political factions squared off—and it was cut to fit their philosophical bents. Official accounts would change or be distorted to suit the ideological or political agenda of the clique in power. Autobiographies, history books and even museums presented only one side of a story—the victor's side, of course. But winners might be losers in the blink of an eye, leaving behind competing versions of history that required much sifting and suspicion. People were erased and un-erased from documents and photographs. Even paintings were carefully retouched to present the politically acceptable interpretation of history that prevailed at the time.

During my early trips around China, when I visited museums in Beijing and other towns and cities, I noticed again and again that the copies of archival photographs on display did not match the originals: the faces of a number of officials had been deleted. In August 1971, I visited the museum in Yan'an, Mao's military base in northwest China from which he led the communist Red Army to victory. Among the heroes shown in the display was Lin Biao, who was the defense minister and the Chairman's designated successor. He was hailed as a "military genius" and a model Maoist. In September 1971, however, Lin reportedly staged a failed coup and died in a plane crash while trying to flee to the Soviet Union. When I revisited the museum in 1972, Lin had been air-brushed from the photographs on display. He was rewritten as an arch-villain and traitor. Learning the history of China was like watching a magician dipping into a box of props. Now you see it, then presto, everything was gone or transformed by sleight of hand.

Apart from all this hocus-pocus, all history courses—not just Chinese history—were steeped in ideological verbiage and viewed through a Marxist-Leninist-Maoist perspective. Modern

European and American history, for example, began with the 1871 Paris Commune, the radical socialist government that briefly ruled the French capital after the collapse of the Second French Empire. The Manifesto of the Paris Commune was required reading for the course ("The communal revolution... begins a new era of experimental, positive, scientific politics"). It was like discovering communism's days of creation. The Paris Commune dovetailed with contemporary works of Karl Marx, the growth of the global workers' movement, the transition from capitalism to imperialism, and, eventually, the birth of Leninism, and the various Russian revolutions.

At Beida, a syllabus on political economy asked us to master Marxist jargon like the "means of production," "production relations," and "law of value." Students were expected to understand the socialist interpretations of concepts like capital formation, monopoly, and oligopoly, as well as concepts such as "to each according to one's labor." We were urged to contemplate questions like: "Why do we say communism is an inevitable historical development?" and "How can we fight for the great ideal of communism?"

The typical professor in Beida followed what some educators called the "empty bottle" approach to teaching. Students were regarded as empty bottles and teachers filled them up with knowledge by lecturing. The professors talked while students listened and took copious notes. Tests and exams were conducted to gauge how much learning had been transferred and retained by students. It was a painful process. We also called it "tianya shi jiaoyu" — teaching the force-fed Peking duck way, a reference to how farmers around the city raised the birds destined for roasting in Beijing's restaurants.

Doing well academically in any Beida course required memorizing arcane terms and phrases about socialism then regurgitating them when prompted by professors. Academic competition was keen; many students vied to prove who was best at this kind of rote learning. But most of the time, we spat out many of the answers on cue without knowing what they meant.

In public, the professors had to profess fealty to the Communist Party line – and make sure it was impressed on their students via the curriculum. In private conversations, however, many would criticize the excesses of the Cultural Revolution and cast doubt on the conventional interpretations of Marxism. They were critical of the mass campaigns of the recent past, during which Red Guards screamed slogans, waved the Little Red Book and sang The East is Red. But most professors, particularly the more senior ones, were ever watchful and anxious of what they said, carefully gauging the direction of the political winds. Stray words had led to so much suffering during the Cultural Revolution only a few years before.

Many of the younger teachers were more relaxed and open, not requiring rote recitation from their students. Unlike the older professors, they could make their lectures come alive and vibrant. Among them was Wang Xiaoqiu, a Shanghai native who was one of the youngest Beida faculty members when the Class of '77 enrolled. Wang was an expert on the two Opium Wars between the Qing Dynasty and Britain, the first in the early 1840s and the second in the 1860s. He was also a leading scholar on the May Fourth Movement in 1919, a galvanizing protest against the partitioning of China by Japan and the Western imperialist powers.

Wang was an unassuming, gregarious lecturer. He spoke in a conversational manner, not in the stiff declamatory style used by some of his counterparts. He spiced his lectures with anecdotes that held our interest instead of rattling off dates and official interpretations of historical events. Most importantly, he would note if there were conflicting versions or views of what actually happened.

In most other classes, free discussions were not encouraged, and asking a professor to explain a concept or detail was rare. Indeed, having anything close to an argument with a "*jiaoshou*" — the venerable term for professor — was considered to be impolite. Things, however, were different in Wang's class. He usually made sure there were ten minutes when he could answer questions or allow for debate. Many years later, Wang told me: "We had to reform teaching methods step by step so we could interact with students."

Aside from Wang Xiaoqiu, I had some other professors who were not straitjacketed by fear and the chains of traditional pedagogy. I enjoyed listening to the lectures of Deng Guangming, an expert on the history of the Song Dynasty from the 10th to 13th centuries, who spoke in a mix of modern and classical Chinese, and whose erudition prompted me to read more deeply into the period. There was Zhang Zhilian, a Francophile and leading expert on European history, who provided the Chinese view of European history but buttressed it with citations from primary source materials, which he had read in their original languages. Zhou Nanjing, an overseas Chinese who returned to China from Indonesia in the 1950s, deepened my limited knowledge of Southeast Asian history, a subject largely ignored in Philippine schools that rather focused on the history of the United States and Europe.

For many of my classmates, even a little glimpse into the unofficial versions of history, was a revelation. "Our eyes were opened for learning beyond the party lines that we were fed with during the earlier formative years," said Jiang Wenran, a global history major and another of my roommates. "We not only remembered historical facts and events but also learned to think deeply on historical and contemporary issues, including the Chinese systems and politics."

But, in that period right after the Cultural Revolution, students could only go so far looking into contemporary Chinese history. The freshness of events and their sensitivity made any investigation at that point a problem, and it remains a conundrum even today. When I visited Professor Wang after his retirement some three decades after I had graduated from Beida, he said the Cultural Revolution remained a perplexing topic of research. "It's now time to straighten things out, clarify the facts and draw lessons. Why did the Cultural Revolution break out? What was Mao thinking? Why did so many people worship him? Why did it turn into a fanatical movement? What damage did it bring to China's society, economy and culture? We have begun to do some research and analysis but still not enough." Many records are not reliable by today's standards, he said. "We used to say that historical analysis depends on records and archival materials. But many of those from the Cultural Revolution period are unreliable, slanderous and even fabricated."

In the Philippines, we adore basketball and play anywhere we can set up a hoop. I'm not particularly tall but like many Filipinos, I have more than basic skills in dribbling and shooting baskets. And so I was very proud to be recruited as a member of Beida's first varsity basketball team since the restoration of *gaokao*. We practiced from 4 to 6 p.m. After practice we all rushed to the cafeteria to get food before they closed. Each time we practiced or played a game we got one yuan in food allowance. That was a considerable sum of money at that time.

I was with the team for three years. My Chinese teammates came from all the departments: history, international relations, law, physics, math and computer science. We also came in various sizes, heights and levels of skills. I was the only foreigner and also the shortest player.

Tang Wenfang, our 6'4" starting center, recalled the historic team — and my part in it — in an online post in 2015:

"In our basketball team, we hung out most closely with Jimi, a student from the Philippines. He was the shortest among us, but he ran fast and was physically very fit, with quick reflexes. Jimi was from the history department. Initially his Chinese was not very good but after interacting with us for years, his Chinese improved quickly. He even learned to say political lingos, as well as various curse words. Everyday he'd spout out slangs like "gemenr" [bro].... He often taught us English. He got along well with everyone and never vented anger at others–except the one time when I saw him lose his cool. That was when we played against the varsity team of People's University. Because the other team's player got flagrantly rough, players started pushing and shoving. Although small, Jimi along with another Beida teammate charged onto the court, shouting in Chinese, 'I'm gonna kill you, tiny rabbit!'"

I don't remember ever saying that. But I remember winning that fiercely-contested match.

In 1979, our Beida team bested both Tsinghua University and People's University in the final round of the All-Beijing College Basketball Championship. In the summer of 1979, our team traveled to Chengdu, the capital of Sichuan Province, to represent Beijing in the first ever All-China Collegiate Basketball Championship, the equivalent of the NCAA championship in the U.S. For three weeks, we practiced and played together. We did well in the preliminary round but lost a close match in the semifinals. We placed third.

Beida students worked hard in the classroom and, outside of the stifling oversight of the close-minded professors, they engaged in open and spirited debate among themselves. Always, the competition was keen and the day-to-day grind unrelenting. A few students failed to measure up to Beida's standards and were unable to withstand the academic and peer pressure. Gao Mingguo, a classmate in the archeology department, arrived in Beida with excellent credentials, having scored among the top ten in the *gaokao* in his home province of Ningxia, an arid and desolate western region. He belonged to the local Communist Youth League—a key step in political advancement—and was regarded as a promising future leader. But after one semester, Gao had difficulty keeping up with his studies. He had to take four make-up exams to avoid expulsion but failed them all. He fell into a deep depression. Concerned that Gao needed more space to himself, several of his roommates vacated their eight-to-a-room living situation, moving to other accommodations so their troubled friend would have to deal with just one roommate. But his depression did not lift. One day, Gao just vanished. "Our whole class searched all over the campus, checked every possible place, even the air-raid tunnels," said one classmate. Two weeks later, a couple of German-language students found Gao's bloated body in Weiming Lake.

Life in Beida was not all academic work. In the evenings and on weekends, students organized lectures, poetry reading and informal talks by visiting academics and experts. They also curated movies screened in school cafeterias, as well as live performances by local or visiting entertainers. The Drama Club, formed mostly by Class'77 and Class '78 students, even staged the Greek play "Oedipus Rex" in Mandarin. In the school's auditorium, students listened to speeches by visiting heads of state, like the Spanish president, and to lectures by noted musicians, like China's foremost female conductor Zheng Xiaoying, who talked on classical music appreciation. These activities did not always have the official imprimatur of the university, but school officials tolerated them to keep the students occupied.

But nothing captured the students' extracurricular spirit more than dancing.

Once banned as a form of bourgeois decadence, social dancing gradually grew in popularity among the Chinese after Mao died in 1976. Initially, city folks danced in the privacy of their homes, unsure if the pastime was politically correct. That changed in Spring of 1978. As in the past, political elites and invited guests gathered in the Great Hall of the People, next to Tiananmen Square, to celebrate the Lunar New Year. This time, the officially sanctioned festivities included ballroom dancing!

I'd been invited to the "gala event" by a friend from the China Friendship Association and, to my surprise, we were encouraged to join in. I found myself pushed onto the dance floor to dance with a Chinese girl, whom I'd just met. Improbably, we waltzed under the gaze of massive portraits of Marx, Engels, Lenin and Mao. Days later, newspapers began to publish pre-Cultural Revolution photographs of Mao and other top Communist leaders indulging in ballroom dancing. Soon, students in *Beida* and other colleges began spreading the word that it was now fine to tango in socialist China.

Zhang Feifei, a *Beida* freshman in 1979, still remembers her "surprise and shock," when as a high school senior, she witnessed men and women locked in embrace while ballroom dancing. "It made me a bit uncomfortable," she recalled when I caught up with her in a 2015 *Beida* reunion. By the time she enrolled in the school's law department, she said, "I was ready to try dancing, except that I had never danced, ever."

Then, one night, she and Li Bo, a fellow member of the women's basketball varsity team, chanced upon two friends from the men's varsity basketball team.

"Elegant music was playing from a boombox and they invited us to dance, but we said we did not know how, so they started to teach us, step by step," Feifei recalled. "We were awkward at first but we got better. This was my first ballroom dance, in the gym with three people." She said, "I got hooked on dancing."

Many conservatives in university administration still frowned on public dancing. But the revived *Beida* never banned it. Said Zhang Manling, a Class of '77 student of Chinese language and literature: "I can't say the dances were elegant or romantic, but they were frenetic. The point was to have fun and defy taboo. The *Beida* spirit was, if you ban dancing, the more we dance." Zha Jianying, a member of the Class of '77 who now writes for the New Yorker recalls, "I went to every single one of the dances. Everybody went to the dances."

On the weekends, our cafeterias became dance halls. In the winters, they were packed with students who kept warm by keeping on their thick cotton-padded coats and scarves as they waltzed and tangoed to music from a scratchy phonograph. As the music went boom cha cha, boom cha cha, the school's Communist Party handlers watched in the background — but did not interfere.

But I was distracted at the time. I had fallen in love again.

I met Wenjing (not her real name) at a dance party. I thought she was Filipina and told her so. She took it as a compliment. We waltzed. That's how it began.

Dance parties had become a bit of a craze after the end of the Cultural Revolution.

The party where I met Wenjing was off-campus and involved other schools. It took place during the Lantern Festival, marking the end of the two-week celebration of the lunar new year. It was 1979 and the Year of the Sheep — a symbol of equanimity, calm, and everybody getting along. There were already auspicious signs. China's parliament had just sent a conciliatory message to Taiwan, which Beijing regards as a renegade province, proposing an exchange of visits and direct transport and tourist links. The U.S. and China formally resumed diplomatic relations. Deng Xiaoping was poised to embark on a historic visit to America. The Chinese public was effusive and expectant: many in Beijing celebrated with firecrackers, which had also returned after being banned by the Red Guard. There were dinner parties everywhere, with sumptuous meals not seen in years and glasses of beer and *maotai*, a 65-proof sorghum liquor.

Our Lantern Festival *wuhui* (dance soiree) was held at the home of Xiao Zhang, a friend studying engineering at Tsinghua University. He was one of the "princelings" — what ordinary people called the scions of families prominent in the party and who enjoyed special privileges and perks, like access to luxurious housing and chauffeured cars. Thanks to his father's senior position in the government, his family lived in an elegant pre-Communist compound with a courtyard, a few kilometers from the Forbidden City. It had a large living room that was perfect for dancing.

The guests were divided almost equally between foreigners and Chinese, but everyone studied in Beijing colleges. With a boom-box, we played cassette tapes of songs ranging from *O Sole Mio* and *Auld Lang Syne* to Johann Strauss's *Blue Danube* waltz. We discovered that the rhythms of Guangdong music, with the mewling of its traditional string instruments, were perfectly suited to the foxtrot. Just five years before, we would all have been arrested for propagating "bourgeois trash" and for playing *mimi zhiyin* — sentimental music that saps revolutionary will. I'm sure there's a way to dance to *Sailing the Seas Depends on the Helmsman*, a paean to Chairman Mao's greatness — but it wouldn't have been fun.

With most of the folks at the party just learning how to dance, there was a good mix of the graceful and the clumsy. I tried to keep track of my cadence to avoid stepping on my partner's feet. And vice versa. But everyone danced. And then someone shouted: "How about *di-si-ke*?"

That would be disco. Since no one knew what disco was, I was volunteered as the night's disco coach. I improvised and told the crowd: "The best way to learn disco? Dance what we Filipinos call *maski paps*." That was a contraction for dancing *maski papano*, or "any which way" as long as you swing with the beat. The Chinese were intent on choreography, but disco dancing could spell freeform!

Amid all of this, I saw Wenjing walk in. (Out of respect for her privacy, I've changed her name and other minor details.) She stood out because she was dressed in a red and white polka-dot dress, the bold pattern an unusual look at a time Chinese were still skittish about standing out in the crowd. She flashed sweet smiles with her big dark eyes. And she asked me to dance. Not disco. But a waltz.

She'd just turned twenty-three and spoke near-perfect English, with an American twang. Most Chinese of her generation spoke with a British accent, acquired from tuning in to Follow Me, a beginners' English program that aired on state-run radio and TV stations virtually every day. She was a senior undergrad at the Beijing Normal University, majoring in English and literature.

Some of her teachers were "foreign experts" from North America and the U.K.

Like most Chinese of her generation, she had spent a year or two working in the countryside in southern China after completing high school. She joined the army briefly and passed the *gaokao* in 1977. She wanted to become a journalist or a diplomat.

"But I still need to improve my English," she said. "Perhaps you can help me?"

She needed little help, but I was smitten. "Of course!" I nodded.

"You could pass for a Filipina," I said, noting that her complexion was darker than most Chinese women. I meant it as a compliment — nostalgic for the beauty of the women I grew up with — and Wenjing said she was flattered. Perhaps, she said, she had Malay features because her parent's hometown is in the southern city of Xiamen, which, as the bird flies, is actually closer to Manila (though first you have to cross the sea) than it is to Beijing.

I told her she also reminded me of Maria, the female lead character of *West Side Story*, who was played by Natalie Wood, a Russian-American made up to look Puerto Rican. When I was in the Philippines, I saw the 1961 film adaptation of the American musical in the movie house and repeatedly listened to its soundtrack on vinyl.

Wenjing had not heard of the musical, so I ended up telling her about it: the tragic love story of two teenagers from different ethnic groups caught in the middle of a rivalry between White and Puerto Rican street gangs in New York City. Wenjing immediately guessed what inspired it: Shakespeare's *Romeo and Juliet*. I told her that one of my favorite songs from the show was "Tonight," a duet sung by Maria and her beloved Tony. I hummed a few lines: "Tonight, tonight, it all began tonight. I saw you and the world went away..."

We danced a little more and then mingled with the rest of the party. But we somehow never got too far from each other. As the party wound down, she agreed to give me her home phone number. I realized she was from a privileged background. In the 1970s, only senior officials had telephone lines installed in their homes. I jotted it down, ripped a page from my notebook and wrote down my dormitory's communal phone number followed by "Room 346", where I lived. The next day, I phoned her. She was waiting for my call.

China had changed dramatically since 1976. While people possessed a deep sense of decorum, public displays of affection were no longer taboo. Wenjing and I did not have to worry about getting accosted by Militia Men, or by the *malie lao taitai* — Marxist-Leninist biddies with their red armbands — who were assigned to report behavior that broke with "socialist morality". We could now hold hands, exchange sweet nothings or even steal kisses in public.

More importantly, the prohibition on Chinese-foreigner liaisons was gone. Intermarriage was now legal. Almost as soon as the first *gaokao* class of students, *Beida* had formally approved of the marriage of a French student and her Chinese boyfriend. It was one of the first such unions in China since the start of the Cultural Revolution in 1966.

Dates with Wenjing were much less fraught than sneaking out with Hai Ou. The pressure was off; things felt more normal. One of our meetings was so-so because it involved a forgettable movie. Another was intriguing. We met up at the Foreign Languages Bookstore in Wangfujing, Beijing's main shopping district. There, we were allowed into a small room restricted to Chinese citizens because it displayed pirated copies of Western books. They were all marked *neibu* – "for internal consumption only". Most of the people browsing were foreign language students, teachers and translators. I was with Wenjing and felt that the store clerks assumed I was Chinese too.

Our favorite spot for a rendezvous was Jingshan Park, which sits on a man-made hill in the center of Beijing. It is not huge by Chinese standards, but it is charming and lush most of the year because it is lined with pine and cypress trees and dotted by gilded pavilions and gazebos. At the top of the hill is a pavilion that overlooks the Imperial Palace, also known as the Forbidden City, and offers an elevated perspective on the capital. It also echoes with tragic history: an emperor hanged himself from a tree on the hill as Beijing fell to rebel forces in the 17th Century. Soon after, the Manchus, an ethnic minority from the northeast, founded the Qing dynasty and replaced the Ming, the last native Chinese imperial dynasty. Wenjing and I typically met in the park in late afternoons, just as the sun began to come down, bathing the Imperial Palace's yellow tiled-roofs and crimson walls with soft, fading light.

Wenjing was often at her parents' well-appointed home on weekends but occasionally she'd stay on campus in the cramped room she shared with three classmates. If all her classmates were out shopping or sightseeing, we'd take advantage of the freedom and make love on her bunk bed.

And then schoolwork and final exams kept us apart. For several weeks from May through June, Wenjing and I kept in touch by periodic phone calls but we rarely saw each other. I was also focused on practicing with *Beida*'s varsity basketball team. Our team had finished No. 1 in Beijing's collegiate basketball tournament, defeating archrival Tsinghua. As champions, we were set to represent the city in the All-China University Basketball Championships, the first nationwide games since

1966, the start of the Cultural Revolution.

In June, my teammates and I took the train to Chengdu, Sichuan's capital city, where the tournament would take place. It was a time for the team — and guys — to bond; it was a diversion from Wenjing. But there was hardly a day I didn't think of her.

We arrived in Chengdu a week before the tournament to familiarize ourselves with its climate, food and tournament venues. I had a great time exploring the city with my pals. I wrote to Wenjing twice — the first time, a post card scribbled, "Wish you were here with me." The second was a letter sharing my impressions of Chengdu and how my team was doing in the national championships. In the semifinals, however, we lost a close game to a scrappy team from northern Liaoning province. In the end, we placed third overall, after besting the other semifinalist.

A few days later, we were back in Beijing, triumphant with the third-place trophy and individual medals. I got back to my *Beida* dormitory, exhausted and sleep-deprived but feeling especially giddy. I could see Wenjing again.

The next morning, I was awakened by a loud announcement blaring out from the dormitory's in-house loudspeaker.

"Room 346! Room 346! .... Telephone call."

It was the hoarse voice of Lao Liu, one of our dorm's gatekeepers who was standing in for Old Man Zhang, in guttural Mandarin. The gatekeepers picked up the calls that came through the communal phone and then would flick on the intercom's loudspeaker to shout out the room number of the person wanted. Everyone knew who was being summoned. There was no privacy. I became notorious for being the dorm-mate who got the most phone calls.

I pulled myself up from bed and rushed down from my third-floor room to take the call. It was Wenjing, as I expected. I started to tell her the news that we placed third and of the wonderful time I'd had in Chengdu when she cut me short.

"We need to meet soon," she said, sounding exasperated. "We need to talk."

"Why?" I asked. "What happened?"

"It's a long story. I'll tell you when we meet. Tomorrow, same place?"

That would be Jingshan Park.

She came dressed in a white blouse and black skirt. We hugged, kissed and started chatting in Chinese. She listened intently as I recounted my Sichuan adventures, the team's victories and travails. She smiled and nodded at all the details I spun out in Mandarin.

Then abruptly she spoke in English.

"Something happened in my life recently, while you were in Chengdu," she said haltingly. "I cannot tell you the whole story, it's complicated, but I am now forced to make a decision that involves my long-term plans, my career, maybe my future." She took in a deep breath and continued: "I am leaving China soon to study in the United States. We have to break up. I'm sorry."

"What?" I blurted out. "What do you mean 'break up'?"

"Break up," she mumbled, staring at me. "I'm so sorry I had to do this." She was tearing up.

We did not speak for several minutes, just holding hands and staring. She tilted her head, resting it on my shoulder. All I could see was the huge expanse in front of me, the Forbidden City and the city's largely flat skyline. The sun was setting.

When she finally spoke, she explained what had happened. While I was away, she'd met an elderly American professor who visited her school to give lectures. For days, she served as his interpreter. She impressed him and before he left Beijing, he offered to get her a scholarship in an American university — a rare, life-changing opportunity.

"Really?" was the only word I could say. I was furious but I held my tongue. She was choosing career opportunity over love, I thought.

She pulled me over and locked me in a tight embrace, whispering in my ear: "I'm so sorry. I love you and I wish we had met in another place and another time."

The night descended and we parted ways as Jingshan Park shut down.

Several weeks later, in early autumn of 1979, I joined a group of Wenjing's relatives and friends at the Beijing airport to see her off for Boston. I did not get a chance to talk to her privately. All I could do was wish her "all the best" along with everyone else.

My anger had become self-pity. I was once again left behind after another farewell. And another broken heart. How can one person have so much bad luck in life and love? I was condemned to indefinite political exile in China because of the dictatorial, undemocratic government of Ferdinand Marcos in the Philippines. It had kept me from my homeland and being close to my family. My two great love affairs had led nowhere. I was alone. It felt so unfair.

8

ROOMIES

ON CAMPUS, one could almost tell which schoolmates were going to be the stars of the future. Bo Xilai stood out not only because he was tall and handsome but, even in an olive-green Mao suit, he exuded the charisma that would fuel his later political career — and eventually make him a target for rivals, including Xi Jinping. He would go on to run a major city and two provinces so successfully that he was promoted to the Politburo, the body which set the policies of the Communist Party itself. Then there was Li Keqiang, who would go on to become Premier of China. He did not project his personality the way Bo did. Enrolled in the newly-revived law department, he was much more circumspect — and yet everyone knew he was going places because of his quiet intensity.

I became a bit of a campus celebrity myself in my junior year. Not only was I the only foreigner on the men's varsity basketball team, but I also appeared on China Central Television's weekly program English on Sunday as a curiosity — someone who was non-Chinese who spoke fluent Mandarin and sang English songs.

Millions of Chinese nationwide watched English on Sunday because it was one of few programs which offered English language lessons. Radio and television in the late 1970s doubled as the country's biggest classroom, teaching languages, science, and math every day. Our one-hour afternoon program featured cut-and-dry language practice drills and lectures, teaching English words and phrases and explaining rules on grammar. It also offered a window to the outside world and whetted the audiences' curiosity about the cultures beyond China's borders.

To freshen up the popular program, the show producers decided to add a series of ten shows, each featuring an English song. They scrambled to find amateur singers and I was one of those recruited to form a kind of "gang of four" who belted out old-fashioned tunes like "Clementine", "Red River Valley", "Jamaica Farewell" and "Que Sera Sera". Only two on the playlist of ten songs qualified as contemporary: "Puff the Magic Dragon" and "El Condor Pasa". One song, "Where Have All the Flowers Gone", failed to make the censor's cut because the narration spoke of the song's anti-Vietnam War message as its historical backdrop. By that time, China's "fraternal" relations with Vietnam, its erstwhile ally, had soured.

We rehearsed several times in the home of Xiao Di, our pianist. We needed a flutist for our rendition of "El Condor Pasa" so we invited a female student at the Central Conservatory of Music. When we thought we were all set, we gathered in the studio of China's Central Television to videotape the ten episodes. The station managers gave us generous talent fees: 10 yuan (equivalent to a week's salary of a government functionary) per person per episode, plus free meals of *baozi* (steamed buns with pork filling) each time we gathered for taping.

During each thirty-minute program, our band of tyros sang each song on tape three times, interspersed with English narrations of the song's synopsis, word definitions and grammatical pointers, all flawlessly delivered in Queen's English by Peng Wenlan, the program's India-born, U.K.-bred host and co-lead singer. We only taped ten programs but, with all the replays, I became a minor celebrity. One of the show producers later told me that among the "fan mail" the TV station received, one letter-writer likened me to a "modern-day Lei Feng whom Chinese youth should emulate," referring to that model PLA foot soldier. A new Lei Feng I was not, but it helped me become popular with the girls. Later, when I started working as a journalist, complete strangers opened up about themselves and their stories, just because they recognized me from TV and felt they knew me.

Every Chinese student I met while I was enrolled in Beida had a story of survival. But I got to know some tales of aspiration and anguish more than others. The most intimate stories came from three men, my roommates at Beida.

Roommate Number 1 was Zhang Jinwei. I met him in late 1977, a few days after I moved into Building 26. He came through the door in the kind of baggy pants everyone wore, but instead of the just-as-baggy Maoist tunic, he had a military-issued jacket, the Chinese equivalent of cool at the time. And he was cool. He walked with a bit of a bounce and liked to ascend stairs with a half-jog. Zhang Jinwei was the son of Zhu Ze, a former diplomat who had become the president of the China Badminton Federation and vice president of the All-China Sports Federation. Sports was the People's Republic's way of cautiously breaking out of isolation and reaching out to the rest of the world. A prime example of this was the ping-pong tournament between U.S. and Chinese athletes that was instrumental to Premier Zhou Enlai meeting Henry Kissinger in 1972—and the thaw in relations between their two countries.

Jinwei was talkative and amiable, being tapped into the "*xiaodao xiaoxi*" grapevine of political gossip about the privileged kids of Communist officials. He always had the backstory on almost any big government conference or what was significant about the appointment of a new official, or where banned films were being surreptitiously screened "for internal consumption." He was keen to get me to help him learn English. I was pleased that he spoke Mandarin with a hint of a Beijing accent, which meant he could help me improve my spoken Chinese. Also, the fact that he was a Beijing resident meant I could have our room to myself when he went home on weekends!

I'm not sure why Beida chose him to be my first roommate. Typically, the Chinese students picked to room with foreigners were members of the Communist Party or the Communist Youth League — politically reliable cadres. They would help ensure that the foreigners remained "safe" — in other words, they'd keep an eye on the outsiders and made sure they behaved. Jinwei was a party member, but I strongly doubt that was his assignment.

People at Beida would eventually describe us as a pair of "*huobao*," which the dictionary translates as "funny men" but, in our case, "young men on steroids" would be more appropriate. Jinwei, was a fierce rebounder in basketball and a sharpshooter, and he was recruited for the varsity team a while before I was. We learned to perform songs together, including a duet about friendship between a Han Chinese and a member of one of China's many ethnic minority groups. For our performances, I played the guitar, which was then exotic and attention-grabbing. The instrument had once been banned as a symbol of foreign bourgeois culture. Few Chinese knew how to make music with it.

But Jinwei and I had one other thing in common: neither of us had to take the *gaokao* to get into Beida. He was one of the *gong-nong-bing* or "worker-peasant-soldier" (WPS) students. Technically, he was selected by his *danwei*, that is, his work unit, at the Museum of Chinese History, on the basis of ideological credentials and the recommendations of the group's leaders. He had to be, indeed, a good Communist.

Jinwei, however, wasn't like most members of his WPS cohorts. Though he worked briefly in the army, he was the son of a diplomat, not the offspring of a factory worker or a farmer. The fact that his family worked for the government probably guaranteed that he had access to books. And, because he was well-read, he had the self-confidence to discuss and debate issues in class. He was part of a group of thirty WPS students, ranging in age from twenty to thirty, who were on a special one-year course at Beida—just as the first batch of *gaokao* enrollees were coming in. The advent of *gaokao* not only ended admission by way of party pedigree, recommendation, and government connections, it would turn anyone into a pariah who was suspected of getting into Beida through those means.

That was the unfortunate situation with Wang Yonghu. He passed the *gaokao* in 1977 but only got into a small college in northwest China. In 1978, however, he managed to get transferred to Beida. Soon after, rumors spread insinuating that Wang gained entry to the prestigious school only because he was the son of Wang Renzhong, a revolutionary veteran and a senior Communist Party official in Beijing. Eventually, Yonghu quit the university and went back to his former college because too many of his Beida schoolmates and teachers believed he had been admitted through what was now called "*zouhoumen*"—the practice of "going through the backdoor." For WPS students, it used to be the front door.

When I got to Beida in late 1977, however, the *gaokao* students hadn't yet arrived. Political and bureaucratic foot-dragging and logistical shortcomings delayed the first nationwide exams, finally pushing them back to November-December 1977. New students didn't start enrolling until February 1978. Until then, Beida belonged to WPS students like Jinwei and foreigners like me.

University advisors suggested that I, along with three female freshmen — two from Japan and one from Pakistan — sit with Jinwei's WPS classmates to study mandatory subjects like ancient Chinese history, philosophy and communist party history until the arrival of the *gaokao* students. Those classes were mostly sleep-inducing. Apart from exceptions like Jinwei, the WPS students lacked basic academic knowledge and training. The teachers spent an inordinate amount of time explaining the simplest matters. The students were enthusiastic and diligent and took copious notes during and after classes. But many of them could hardly keep up with the required readings. Some hardly spoke during class discussions.

Jinwei turned out to be the perfect roommate. After school, he helped me with class work, explaining new words and sharing lecture notes. He knew tons of historical trivia because of his job as a guide at the museum, a government-run institution housed in a massive building next to Tiananmen Square. He'd have entertaining asides like the fondness of Tang dynasty men for plump women. Or serious ones, like how the writer Lu Xun was supposedly hounded and harassed by the Kuomintang police.

Jinwei was also with me when I had one of the most important personal experiences in my life in China: my reunion with my parents. In the years since I left, my mother had heard so many rumors about what had happened to me, she didn't know what to believe. "Luding heard stories about Jaime and his companions," my father wrote in his memoirs, that "they were on forced labor in the people's communes; that they were seen in the hills in north Luzon leading a [communist] guerrilla unit, all of which were false."

My parents longed to see me. They also wanted to make sure I was getting an education. With all my siblings through college, my father wrote, "Jaime was the only one of six children who we wished and felt obliged to see through a baccalaureate degree, hence the circumstances gave me occasional moments of failing in my fatherly duties."

Like the Chinese, Filipinos put a premium on education.

In summer of 1977, my parents took early retirement from their government jobs and migrated to the United States, where two of my sisters and a brother had settled. In the summer of 1977, while staying with my sister in New York, my father wrote to the China International Travel Service (CITS) to book a ten-day package tour to China. Obsessed with control and security even then, the Chinese at that point did not allow visitors to enter with only one destination in mind and had them book multiple-city itineraries that they could supervise. I knew they were arriving soon but did not know exactly which date.

"Upon arrival, there were several hours of suspense," my father wrote, recalling coming to Beijing with my mother. "Jaime was nowhere in sight, nor was a representative of the China Travel Service, a car, driver, or interpreter, which were included in the package-tour."

Language differences hampered communication. It turned out that they arrived in Beijing one day before the CITS expected. They had written me a letter to tell me they were coming but it had never reached me.

Finally, someone helped them get into a taxi and taken to the travel service office. "It was raining, damp and humid," my father wrote. "Likewise dampened was my spirit." An agency representative took them to Peking Hotel. "The CITS man was profuse with apologies for the mix-up which was not their fault," my father recalled. "I inquired about Jaime and he promised to send word to him."

It was 6:40 in the evening and my parents were hungry, so they went to the hotel's Chinese restaurant. "About 7:00 p.m. while we were eating, Jaime arrived carrying an overnight bag," my father wrote. "Luding was so intensely carried away that she could not withhold her tears. The waitress, who knew Jaime as her former teacher of English, noticed our tearful reunion and correctly surmised that we were Jaime's parents. It was such a big relief and comfort to be with Jaime after such long separation."

I stayed with my parents at the hotel during their eight days' stay in Beijing.

A few days later, after I had taken my parents to the Forbidden City and the Great Wall, I brought them to Peking University for a campus tour. They visited my dormitory and met my roommate Zhang Jinwei. My father described our dorm as "Spartan" with "just enough space for the beds, study table and for their uniforms and clothing, but livable and probably better than in other dormitories on campus. What we did not fail to notice were the many friends of Jaime and how he was held in high esteem by the head and staff of the Office of Foreign Students of the university."

Father further wrote: "I was more interested in hearing from Jaime about his experience and being physically together rather than seeing the many wonders of the oldest civilization in the history of mankind." But he added, "Jaime's oral English teaching to hotel and restaurant attendants, tour guide and interpreters gained him many friends; was recognized by an employee of the Botanical Garden during our visit." Actually, many of the staff and people we met recognized me because I taught conversational English to various groups in my spare time. It certainly helped impress my father.

The eight days of reunion with my parents came to an abrupt

end. The day they left Beijing, I looked totally transformed. Instead of the blue Mao suit and black cotton shoes, I wore for them what they had brought specially for me: a cream jacket, a brown T-shirt, a pair of tapered jeans and a pair of leather sneakers. I held Inang's hand tightly as we sat in the Peking Airport terminal waiting for Amang to check in luggage and get their boarding passes. We hardly spoke. Amang took out his camera and asked the CITS interpreter to take our picture. Then we hugged tightly and whispered hurried goodbyes.

"Parting was such sweet sorrow when we bade goodbye to Jaime," Amang wrote in his diary. "It was a tearful goodbye for Luding in spite of Jaime's parting words '*huwag kayong mag-alala*' (don't worry)."

They boarded the plane that took them to Guangzhou and, days later, back to the Philippines.

Zhang Jinwei's batch of Worker-Peasant-Soldier students wouldn't graduate till July and overlapped with the *gaokao* students for five months. It was not a happy time. One day in the spring of 1978, a wall poster appeared on campus. Apparently written by a freshman *gaokao* student, the handwritten message disparaged the Worker-Peasant-Soldier cohorts as "country bumpkins" who should not have been allowed to enroll in the university in the first place.

The "country bumpkins" immediately fought back with their own posters. They called the new students elitist and arrogant and denounced the return of the *gaokao* as a "restoration of the bourgeoisie." Putting a premium on test scores, they said, perpetuated social inequality at the expense of the workers. It would create a privileged ivory tower class divorced from the masses and reality. For days, the posters attracted throngs of students who argued the pros and cons of *gaokao* and its effects on the direction of education in China.

School authorities intervened to calm both sides. The posters were soon taken down. In the summer, the WPS students graduated and grudgingly left, mostly to return to their previous jobs as workers, peasants and soldiers. I bade goodbye to Jinwei and my other WPS classmates. There was no graduation ceremony, no big send-off parties, only simple farewell meals and bottles of beer — and a duet or two.

My second roommate was Jiang Wenran. The fall term had just begun in 1978. I was standing in line at the cafeteria, which we called the "Big Dining Hall" — a mockingly grand name because there usually weren't any chairs and we had to stand around a large round table while chowing down. I struck up a conversation with one of the people next to me, Jiang Wenran, a native of the northeastern city of Harbin and a world history major from Class of '77. He said he was an expert at raising chickens because he'd worked at a poultry farm. He could speak a little Russian because Harbin used to have a sizeable community of Russians, but he said I was the first foreigner he had ever met. As luck would have it, Jiang showed up at my dorm room in Building 26 a few days later. He had been assigned to be my new roommate. And, through the years, he and I would become the best of friends.

I started calling him "Xiao Jiang" (Little Jiang) because, even though he was taller than I am, I was five years older. He was gregarious and kinetic, with a quick smile, easily breaking into exuberant guffaws. He was always doing something: visiting friends at their dormitories, stopping by for tea, borrowing books and magazines, making new acquaintances. He eagerly joined in volleyball and basketball pick-up games, even though he wasn't particularly good at sports. And like most of the Class of '77, he had his own epic of survival.

He was the eldest of three children born to mid-level government officials. He was still a toddler when Mao initiated the disastrous "Great Leap Forward," which led to three years of famine in most of China. Xiao Jiang recalls being hungry and unable to get food or attention. By the time he became a teenager, the Cultural Revolution was sweeping the country. "I was too young to be a real Red Guard but old enough to remember what was going on, if not fully understanding things," he told me. He saw Red Guards ransacking the homes of neighbors accused of being capitalists and saw violent fights between radical factions. His mother was labeled by the Red Guards as coming from the landlord class, because her family was ethnic Manchu and therefore members of the ruling class of the last imperial dynasty. She was demoted from doing bookkeeping to working on a production line at a tofu factory.

When Xiao Jiang finished high school in 1972, he and about 800 other kids who graduated at the same time were sent to the countryside for "re-education by the peasants." He was lucky: the farm was not too far from the suburbs of Harbin where his family lived. He raised chickens for five years, "doing farm work while dreaming to build a new socialist countryside," Xiao Jiang recalled with an ironic grin.

Despite the rigors, Xiao Jiang and thirty other young people on the farm formed a "theoretical study group," a sort of Marxist book club. In their spare-time, they read and discussed *Das Kapital* and other communist classics. When the city library partially reopened, they expanded to books on modern history. The activity kept their literacy up but the five years on the farm burned them out physically. The labors had also taken a toll on the ideal of a "new socialist countryside."

Then came 1976, Mao's death, the arrest of the Gang of Four, and Deng's political comeback. By the end of 1977, the *gaokao* was reinstated.

"This was a big deal for my family, especially for my parents," he said. The competition was enormous for admission into Beida and other prestigious universities—with tens of thousands of local kids in his home province of Heilongjiang expected to take the entrance exam. The province was allocated only five to six slots for admission into Beida that year.

His family helped him fill in the forms. They had tough choices to make. Applicants had to put down their first, second and third preferences of schools—ranging from any of the premier national universities to the lesser colleges in the provinces and cities, or even local trade and vocational schools. If an applicant's scores were not high enough for the first choice, he or she could be considered for the second choice. But the officials of that second-choice university had the right to pass on the applicant, picking instead applicants with the same score but who made their university their first preference.

"For many of us, the choice was either to be a farmer for life or to play safe and aim for a college that one could likely get into," Xiao Jiang said. "None of the people from my farm or anyone I knew considered applying for top universities like Beida. Some wished to, but their families persuaded them to play safe."

Xiao Jiang nearly did that. His parents thought he should apply for a university in his native Harbin city to ensure that he could move his "*hukou*" — place of residence—from the suburban chicken farm back to the city. But Xiao Jiang had his own plans. Beida's prestige, he believed, would change his life, and he would take the gamble.

"I wanted very badly to go to the best humanities university in China—Beida, Fudan (in Shanghai) or Nankai (in Tianjin)," Xiao Jiang explained. "I told my parents that for the first time in my life, I would not follow their advice. I had made up my mind that I'd apply for Beida and, if I failed, I would stay home and study for another year and try for Beida again." I am glad that he did.

We developed a close friendship. Soon after the annual three-week winter break started, he was heading home by train and invited me to come along. But I was noncommittal, because I had started to pick up freelance journalism assignments —a good chance to earn extra money and satisfy my passion for reporting.

The week that Xiao Jiang left for home, I had an assignment from a U.S. ski magazine to interview John Norris, an American skiing coach who was hired by the Chinese Sports Ministry to train China's fledgling national ski team. I took a train to Jilin province in northeast China and went to the snow-capped training ground of China's best skiers.

It was the dead of winter in late January. The hills were dotted with pine trees and covered with foot-high snow, perfect for ski training but a curse to a Filipino reporter who had never seen so much snow, much less knew how to ski. I was offered a pair of skis and briefly considered trying them, but promptly brushed the idea aside. What if I broke a leg?

Camera and notebook in hand, I followed on foot the charismatic coach and his eager trainees, a dozen men and women, as they raced over the carpet of snow. Panting heavily, I tried to catch Norris' stern instructions and clever tips. I tried to capture their cross-culture interactions, taking notes and snapping pictures. Three days later, I wrapped up the interviews and planned to head back to Beijing. Then I realized that Jilin is only a few hours' train ride from Harbin, Xiao Jiang's hometown. He did not have a phone, so I had no way to alert him that I was coming. I bought a ticket for an evening train—the earliest available—on the eve of Chinese New Year. At the station, I picked up a bottle of grape wine that the city was famous for. I got off at the Harbin station close to midnight. It was bitter cold, about minus 20°C (minus 4°F). Even though I had put on layers, including a sweater and jacket and overcoat, I felt my hands and feet were virtually frostbitten. I was starving and exhausted from walking because I could not find a taxi. Holding the piece of paper with Xiao Jiang's address, I stopped repeatedly to ask for directions until I finally found his residence. It must have been 1 a.m. by then.

Xiao Jiang was totally surprised when he opened the door. We hugged and burst out laughing. He quickly introduced me to his startled parents and two sisters. It turns out they were midway through the traditional late New Year's Eve dinner, and they immediately sat me down around the dining table—which was laid out with plates of vegetable and meat dishes, still piping hot, bottles of liquor, and piles of fruit. Of course, there were *jiaozi* (steamed dumplings)!

Dumplings are considered a lucky food to ring in the Lunar New Year. They symbolize wealth because they resemble the shape of silver and gold ingots, an ancient form of Chinese currency. There's a belief that the more dumplings you eat on that occasion, the more money you will reap.

Immediately, Xiao Jiang's mother handed me a bowl brimming with bulging dumplings. She told me that they follow a tradition, more common in northern China: when they prepare dumplings, they slip a coin inside one of them. Whoever gets that dumpling will be blessed with an auspicious year. I wolfed down one dumpling after another, dipping them in vinegar and minced garlic.

I'm not sure now if it was totally set up or if it was really my good fortune, but I did get the lucky dumpling. Jiang's family cheered and clapped. And, not long after that nian ye fan (New Year's Eve family dinner), I did have good luck— I got my first job offer to work for Newsweek magazine.

There were rumors at that time that somehow Chinese students assigned to live with foreign students were all screened or selected to monitor their roommates. "That was never the case, at least not in my case," Wenran told me years later. "No one in my department mentioned or assigned such a task. We began as honest-to-goodness roommates."

Xiao Jiang and I loved to goof off and procrastinate over term papers. And we always had time to debate over everything, especially Chinese and Western values. He was prudish — as were the authorities. The university banned students from having romantic or sexual relations — though not everyone abided by the rules. Xiao Jiang and I talked about girls we were interested in all the time. Still, he was shocked that men and women in the West and the other parts of the world could date more than one person at a time — and yet remain respectable. He also was curious about why there was so much wealth and extravagance — and waste of food, water and energy resources — in developed countries. Did they really dump milk into rivers rather than sell it in the market just to keep milk prices from falling, as he had read in some magazine? He thought young people in the West were dangerously materialistic and self-centered, obsessed with personal freedom at the expense of duty to the society.

For Xiao Jiang and the rest of the new students at Beida, the challenge was to soak up as much knowledge as possible to make up for the "lost years," the internal exile spent in farms and factories. The whole Class of 1977, including our classmates Bo Xilai and Li Keqiang, faced the same challenges, and shared the same goal — transcending the past.

The sense of mission was intense, even though what the mission would entail wasn't exactly clear to anyone at all. Students put forth all kinds of advocacies in the intense discussions held in classrooms and in dormitory rooms, but most were vague, long range and without any clear blueprint. More than anything, the students were all searching for knowledge. "Our days began really early in the morning," Jiang remembered. "When I got up in the morning, some of my classmates had already come back from their daily routine reciting English words and phrases while taking a walk. We had this desperate desire to study, quickly, not only about those assigned in class but just about anything we could grab and absorb."

I remember coming back to the dorm one day to find our room bedecked with little bits of paper. Xiao Jiang had decided that four hours a week of English classes wasn't enough for him and that the fastest way for him to improve his vocabulary was by sticking labels on the actual objects around him: "teacup," "chair," "toothpaste," "lamp", "ash tray".

With the focus so fervently on the future, no one complained too much about the inconveniences of the present.

"So many things were new and exciting," Xiao Jiang told me. "We did not care much if our classrooms did not look nice, if we had to stand around dining tables because there were no chairs, or if the cafeteria was not heated in winter."

If the new China required more personal sacrifice, then eating a little more bitterness — the Chinese expression for persevering through difficulties — was worth it. The immediate past had already been painful, but tomorrow could be better if we worked hard enough.

Beida's school policy required a change in Chinese roommates every year or two. "It's to give as many Chinese students the chance to room with you overseas students," explained Huang Daolin, who was the deputy director of the foreign students office. "It was then a coveted privilege, with better dorm facilities and the chance to learn a foreign language."

I knew that by the fall of 1980, Xiao Jiang and I would be separated. Xiao Jiang still credits me with helping him master English and for our frequent debates that helped him appreciate the openness and spirit of the West. He eventually moved to Canada and became a tenured professor of political science, first at Carleton University and later at the University of Alberta. When he married Tanya Casperson, one of the students at Carleton, he asked me to be his best man.

He remembers one thing about that cold Chinese New Year's Eve in Harbin in 1980. As a gift, I brought a bottle of Tonghua grape wine, still rare in China in those days, but amid all the merriment and talk, we forgot to open it. Xiao Jiang told me that his mother "has kept that bottle until today, stored in a cabinet at our home in Harbin, waiting for your next visit."

My third roommate, Li Xiaocong, was four years older than I and so I called him Lao Li—Old Li. But despite that seniority, he got into Beida one year later than I did. By then, he had already spent ten years in Tibet. It was an exotic and remote place to most Chinese. But Lao Li, who was born and raised in the capital in a family of intellectuals, was caught up in the spirit of the Cultural Revolution and, in 1968, at the height of the turmoil, he and eleven students from three high schools in Beijing volunteered to go to Tibet to help with the frontier region's economic development.

The ultra-idealistic teenagers took the arduous multi-day trip to Lhasa, the Tibetan capital, which is nearly 12,000 feet above sea level. As part of their work, they trekked for weeks through Tibetan villages to live with the locals and to improve their own socialist principles by so doing. Communist Party leaders in the area eventually assigned them to work in a farm in the suburbs of Lhasa. Despite his enthusiasm, the years in Tibet were hard. He had to adapt to local customs like eating tsamba—barley bread— and drinking tea with yak milk. Yet, he still retained a sense of romanticism about the endeavor. It required endurance and grit, and he was proud to have been part of it, to have overcome vicissitudes to survive.

In 1970, Li and twenty other young people from Beijing joined a team of engineers organized by the Chinese Ministry of Petroleum to do field work prospecting for oil in Tibet. "I started as a trainee and for six years worked as an oil-drill operator and a diesel truck driver," Lao Li said. It was one of the government's pipedreams. The Chinese never found enough petroleum in Tibet to make the enterprise worthwhile. "Later I was moved to work in the team's chemical laboratory as technician," he said. He went on field trips to several remote mountainous areas, most of which were about 15,500 above sea level. He was still working in Tibet when the government announced the revival of the *gaokao*. He signed up for the second round of tests and got in on Tibet's Beida quota.

For all of his fervent teenage nationalism, Li was fascinated by Western music, including all the Beatles songs I would sing with my guitar. He didn't sing too well himself, but he loved "Yesterday." Years later, when he made his first trip to England, he made it a point to visit Liverpool because it was the home of the Fab Four. Bespectacled and portly, Lao Li spoke in a slow, deliberate manner, parsing his words to be clear and accurate. He was gentle and diplomatic, always finding the gray area when discussing controversial issues. That is probably why our history class selected him as class monitor. He always found a way to defuse heated debates, especially about the excesses of the Cultural Revolution. Invariably, Lao Li advised both sides to consider each other's position calmly, reminding them that it was a Marxist virtue to be able to see both sides of an argument.

He could go through cryptic classic Chinese texts seemingly without effort, a reflection of a deep and immediate knowledge of the key sources of Chinese history from all periods, an astonishing feat considering that the record of the country's past goes back more than 3,000 years. He specialized in history and geography in his undergraduate courses and later in graduate studies. Lao Li would eventually become a sought-after lecturer on the authenticity of old maps and artifacts. Museums in England, the Netherlands, the United States, and Taiwan have commissioned him to assess, date or critique ancient maps and documents in their archives.

All of which meant that Lao Li was an excellent roommate to have on hand to help me with my history requirements. He was especially helpful with my graduation thesis.

My research topic was the "December 9th Movement", a mass protest led by students that broke out in Beijing in 1935, during the struggle between the Nationalist government and the Communists, with an array of regional warlords in play as well. On that date, a small phalanx of students from a number of the city's colleges, including Tsinghua and Peking University, took to the streets to press the Chinese government to take a more aggressive stance against the Japanese invasion. Defying sub-zero temperatures and police bayonets and fire hoses, the students marched and chanted: "Down with Japanese Imperialism!" "Stop the civil war", "Unite against Japan!" This protest snowballed into a patriotic movement that eventually united all the Chinese against the Japanese invasion.

My thesis was simple: although short-lived and far from massive, the 1935 student movement was a turning point for the Communist campaign to rule China. After the movement was suppressed by the Nationalist government, many of the student-activists trekked to Yan'an, the mountainous stronghold of Chairman Mao and his Communist army who had regrouped there. Educated and highly idealistic, they strengthened Mao's efforts with their energy and talents. When the Communists swept to victory over the Nationalists in 1949, many of these young cadres played critical roles in building the bureaucracies of the new Communist regime. They later took up senior positions in the government, the Communist Party and the army.

The subject was also appealing to me personally because I had been a student activist in the Philippines — though the situations and historical perspectives, of course, were quite different.

When I started my research in 1981, many of the December 9 veterans were still alive and active in the party, military and government. The challenge was how to compile their names and where to find them. This was decades before computerized search engines and many archival documents were classified as confidential or "for internal circulation only." Lao Li and other friends were key to drawing up a December 9 Who's Who list. I tracked down more than a dozen of them and requested interviews, and most of them agreed.

Their accounts helped me flesh out my graduation paper, which ended up being 10,000 Chinese characters long. My professors liked it, noting "The theory and viewpoint of the thesis is basically correct." They appreciated the investigative work, too. "Archival materials are rich, especially because the author, based on research of historical documents, conducted interviews and surveys among participants and eyewitnesses. The author uses new materials and raises new viewpoints." I got a grade of 89 out of 100.

For that, I was grateful to Lao Li. I held his fortitude and his scholarship in high regard. But I also admired his ability to balance out an academic life with what looked to be a happy home. In 1973, while living and working in Tibet, he married Zhan Ruoying, a girl from Beijing whom he met on that first idealistic adventure to the faraway region. They were in Tibet together when he decided to take the *gaokao*. When he passed, they moved back to Beijing together. By then, the couple had a son Li Nian, born in November 1976. As he pursued his studies at Beida, Lao Li, always made certain he spent the weekends in his Beijing home with his wife and son.

Admission to Beida did not, of course, guarantee personal bliss like Lao Li's. Indeed, the pursuit of academic and professional ambitions sometimes led to heartbreak and tragedy. Such was the story of Tang Wenfang, the classmate who studied English in part by reading Masters and Johnson's *Human Sexual Response*.

Wenfang had been happy as a factory worker. He had his benefits and a girlfriend named Yan. But his mother disapproved of Yan and wanted her son to get into college. He agreed on two conditions. One, if he passed, he would major in English, and not in biology or medicine as his mother preferred. Two, she had to accept his relationship with Yan. His mother agreed to both. And so, Wenfang studied day and night for the *gaokao*, with Yan cooking his meals and doing his laundry to allow him to focus on his studies. He passed. Soon, the couple began talking about getting married, renting an apartment, having children.

Once he had settled into Beida, however, Wenfang's worldview changed. "When I started to plunge into the new and lively world of the university," Wenfang recalled, "I began to feel fewer sparks between us." There was one crucial factor. Yan was sweet and affable but had barely any education. "One day, I told her that I wanted to end our relationship. She was crushed and refused to accept this. She promised that she would become a better person and make our life more romantic." But he wanted the relationship to end.

Yan accused Wenfang of destroying her life because he took her virginity, declaring it was immoral for him to dump her just because his life was getting better.

"I told Yan that virginity and marriage were not necessarily linked in the modern world," Wenfang said, citing what he learned in *Human Sexual Response*.

"Forget the stupid book!" Yan screamed. "We are Chinese and we should behave in the Chinese way!"

Wenfang felt miserable. But he noticed similar disruptions in the lives of people around him. The Chinese media was increasingly filled with stories of people who went to college and divorced their spouses or broke up with their girlfriends or boyfriends. "I was deeply ashamed for breaking up with Yan," Wenfang said, "but I could not help but think about the serious difficulties that faced us in the future."

"Three months into my freshman year, I received news that Yan had been found dead in her apartment. The cause was an accidental gas leak. She was twenty-four."

He could not muster the courage to attend the funeral, only going to the cemetery later, alone. He stood before the urn containing her ashes. "I prayed for her happiness in heaven and begged for her forgiveness."

9

CONTAMINATED BY DEMOCRACY

I REMEMBER the sameness and uniformity that ruled China when I first arrived in 1971, the singularity of thought, policed sometimes violently by the Red Guards, the drab green-and-khaki Mao suits that everyone wore, disguising even gender in the name of egalitarianism. The Cultural Revolution sought to bring everyone—in mind, spirit, and appearance—down to the same level. And for a while, practically everyone in China was cowed into believing that such conformity was a virtue, that the ideal state of the people was as a single-minded, mass organism that the ideologues in power could bend to their will, without protest, and without complaint.

But by 1979, just three years after the death of Mao, China had entered a state of cultural and economic flux—and also of political ferment. Social dancing was just a reflection of the country loosening itself from the constraints of Maoist prudery. That such an audacious form of bourgeois pastime was being allowed was thrilling. And it would not be long before the Chinese elite and their children held periodic dances, switching from foxtrot to the tango and then learning the moves of they called "*di-si-ke*" —that is, disco.

Daily life began to brighten up for ordinary Chinese. Colors other than olive green began to perk up fashion. Pigtails were really the only hairstyle women were allowed during the height of the Cultural Revolution. But, as the Red Guards vanished from sight, some women started to sport pageboy cuts and wavy perms. Bolder ones experimented with the "*bulaji*", the fitted dress.

Ideological fashions began to change too. Without fanfare, my Chinese friends started discarding some of their old baggage. Mao's cult of personality began to fade.

At Beida, starting in the mid-1970s, there were no more obligatory hymns to the Chairman, no more community singing of "The East is Red," that hymn to the Chairman. Gone, too, were the sacred Maoist amulets — the Mao pins, the revolutionary posters, the Little Red Book.

Like all things in China's recent past, the liberalization was mandated from the top. Deng Xiaoping's Four Modernizations had led to an almost immediate improvement in the lives of farmers, who could now sell at least some of their produce for a profit, and of urban dwellers, who could now receive cash bonuses if they produced more than their quota of work at factories. The economic difference was palpable, indeed, visible. Ordinary Chinese for the first time in many years suddenly had disposable income.

There was constant talk of the Three Big Things that people had to have to show their lives were improving. At first, it was a bicycle, a wristwatch and a sewing machine. But as consumer finances surged, so did the list. Over time, the Three Big Things changed to a refrigerator, a washing machine, a TV set. Later, even the name of the list had to expand, becoming the "*san zhuan, yi ting, yi kacha*" (three turns: a bike, a watch, and a washing machine; one listen: a cassette player; and one click: a camera). The amendments kept coming and the expectations kept rising.

The pronouncement that set off this new revolution and the

visible flux in 1979 was a speech delivered by Deng Xiaoping on Dec. 13, 1978. Its title alone was a form of emancipation for the Chinese people: "Liberate Our Minds, Seek Truth from Facts, and Unite to Move Forward." And a country that was used to marching in lock-step, moved forward together into a whole new set of freedoms — and political and cultural churn.

Suddenly, the Chinese were ready to embrace new and foreign things again, freed from Maoist knee-jerk xenophobia. At first cautiously and suspiciously, China opened its door to foreign tourists and to capitalists scouting for new markets and joint ventures. Many Chinese took crash courses in foreign languages, especially English. In 1979, some 10,000 students were sent to study overseas. The pragmatic goal was to "make foreign things serve China, make the past serve the present."

The Central Philharmonic began to play concertos by Liszt and Beethoven, composers who a few years earlier had been denounced as "decadent bourgeois." State-run Radio Peking started to play tunes like Woody Guthrie's "This Land Is My Land" and the Neapolitan standard "O Sole Mio." More and more once-banned Western fare showed up in cinemas, including old classics like Charlie Chaplin's "Modern Times." CCTV, the monopoly state-run television channel spiced up its programming by airing cheaply acquired American TV programs like "Garrison's Guerrillas", a World War II-themed series.

The most controversial liberalization, however, was not officially sanctioned and while widely discussed, was not implemented. It was called the "fifth modernization" — democracy. The discussion about the political system was encouraged by several moves on the part of the government. China rehabilitated thousands of bureaucrats and intellectuals who were once vilified as "Rightists" and "counter-revolutionaries." The government also freed a number of long-imprisoned political dissidents, among them was Li Yizhe, one of three dissidents jailed in 1974 for advocating "socialist democracy and legality." Gradually, there was greater, albeit still limited, discussion on a wide range of topics. In Beida and many university and intellectual circles, the excitement over what these moves meant was immense. Fresh political ideas percolated and were debated. Students and young intellectuals organized discussion groups called "Democracy Salons." They published mimeographed magazines and pamphlets, like *Tansuo* (Exploration), which carried political essays and poetry that questioned the old ideas and practices.

As my schoolmate Zhou Yuan, who was in Beida's English department, recalls, "Some people proposed reforms, like holding People's Congress elections, advocating significant changes in the political system while keeping its basic structure. Others advocated that we learn from the West, basically to copy what some countries had done." And there were other advocacies, Zhou says, "for a more radical kind of reform, as if to do away with the communist model all together."

That was both opportunity and danger. In 1979, many ordinary Chinese decided the atmosphere was right for them to air their grievances, to let the government know what they felt. They took to Big-Character wall posters (*dazibao*) to express themselves, just as they had in the times of the Red Guards a decade before. Ordinary citizens began making public their aspirations on a seven-foot-high brick wall near the Xidan intersection, west of Tiananmen Square and Zhongnanhai, the official headquarters of the Communist Party.

This was the "Democracy Wall" movement, which began in November 1978 and lasted through March 1980. Originally the wall, which flanked a bus depot, was merely a spot where bus schedules were put up, and people used it to pin pleas for help to find lost objects — bicycles, books, bags. Because it was such a hub, the notices began to range wider, with citizens proposing swaps of government-provided housing, for example. Quickly, however, the subject matter became political and the posters proclaimed a wide range of desires and complaints. That attracted greater numbers of people, curious to read about the latest political grievances, even including attacks on government officials and veiled criticism of the late Chairman Mao. Among the posters that stood out was an essay called "The Fifth Modernization" put up by an electrician named Wei Jingsheng, who argued that democracy was as an indispensable reform as Deng Xiaoping's four others: revamping agriculture, industry, science and technology, and national defense. It was the most electrifying public demand to emerge in the post-Mao era. People gathered by the wall just to soak up the feverish political excitement—and to bask in the riskiness of it all, the feeling that the government couldn't possibly allow this ferment to go on. In fact, the government's security apparatus—uniformed and plainclothes police—were already closely monitoring the gatherings.

I rode my Flying Pigeon bike several times over from Beida to Xidan to read the posters, ignoring the advice of friends who worried about my safety. A counselor at school said, "The political situation is very complicated," and warned that the "chaos" could escalate. He told me to be "careful because such a movement could be manipulated and get out of hand."

I hung around to listen to the street-side debates and discussions. Intermittently, some people stood on the wall and extemporaneously gave impassioned speeches. I heard someone call for a public trial of the Gang of Four. Another wished to build a memorial for the Premier Zhou Enlai in Tiananmen Square, next to the one for Chairman Mao. Another person proposed designating the area of the wall in Xidan as a "sacred place" for free speech, just like Hyde Park Corner in London.

In fact, the increasingly public and loud calls for political change emanating from the vicinity of the Democracy Wall were prompting a backlash from conservative elements in the government—indeed, becoming a cudgel they would wield against Deng and his program of economic liberalization. Throughout its long history, China has had prolonged periods of *"luan"* —chaos—and the conservatives would play on such historical fears with the possibility that the Democracy Wall movement would lead to public upheavals and jeopardize government control over order.

Even as reforms spread all over China, the political conservatives who wanted to preserve Maoist and leftist supremacy mounted a vigorous, behind-the-scenes campaign against change. Many of the advocates of retrenchment remained nostalgic for pre-reform egalitarianism. Although they agreed that the system was broken, some conservative officials preferred the old status quo.

The gatherings and extemporaneous protests that grew around the Democracy Wall shocked many of the top leaders of the Communist Party and gave conservatives the ammunition to criticize the reformers. The hardliners branded the protests as a "counter-revolutionary" conspiracy, blaming it on Deng's tolerance for public discussions. These, they argued, allowed unorthodox opinions to spread, especially among the youth. In contrast, there was also the view that Deng used the Democracy Wall, at least for a time, as a way to show the conservatives that people wouldn't tolerate chaos even as they aspired for change.

Deng Xiaoping after a while tightened controls, calling on the people to adhere to his proposed "Four Cardinal Principles of Socialism," which included upholding the paramount leadership of the Communist Party. The Chinese media was directed to call the Democracy Wall gatherings "deviations" and forms of "bourgeois liberalization."

Police arrested several prominent participants, including Wei Jingsheng, who would be sentenced to fifteen years in prison for "counter-revolutionary agitation" and "leaking secrets to foreigners." The amateur magazines that had been a part of the Democracy Wall experience were banned. Poster-writing and political gatherings in Xidan were gradually suppressed, but democratic ideas would continue to bubble up among students, workers, and the intelligentsia.

The conservative backlash against Deng's modernization efforts was not confined to ideology. In 1983, conservatives blamed the rising incidence of corruption and economic crimes — such as bribery, graft, and the embezzlement of public funds — and crass materialism on the spread of "cultural contamination" and foreign ideas seeping into China. This backlash prompted Deng to institute a short-lived campaign against "spiritual pollution."

Amid the crackdown, Beida and the universities remained calm. But many students were angry about the political turn. "That was the first time we felt disappointed with Deng," a classmate told me. But many were still willing to give Deng the benefit of the doubt, that the crackdown was an "expedient measure" that allowed him to maneuver through conservative enemies in high places. Unfortunately, he said, "history proved that the people and the students were wrong." Deng chose political stability over political reform.

Meanwhile, as a foreigner, I bucked the political headwinds and continued my role as promoter of "spiritual pollution." I did, of course, have an audience hungry for such cultural contamination, as embodied in cassettes of English-language pop songs that I kept in constant fresh supply, thanks to my fellow foreign students. I shared these "spiritual pollution" with my Beida classmates and dorm mates. I continued my tutoring in English at Beida and, also at the Beijing Teachers' College. I would spice up my lectures with introductions of foreign ideas and cultures as well as customs and etiquette—enhancing the sense of the forbidden. I introduced my classes to cultural and religious traditions—including Thanksgiving and Halloween, which were largely unknown to the Chinese.

As part of my curriculum's "show-and-tell," I threw a rowdy party or two, including a decadent Halloween party where I asked my Chinese students and other guests to come in costume. They were fairly wild for the still-conservative Chinese. One came as a cowboy; another dressed as an Arab sheik. I wore a body-hugging cheongsam—Cantonese for what in Mandarin is called the *qipao*, a clinging dress with a thigh-high slit. I wore full make-up. The party climaxed with frenetic dancing, led by myself and a few foreign enrollees at Beida. My students tried disco dancing John Travolta-style. They were "chaperoned" of course by the Communist Party commissar assigned to make sure no one truly misbehaved. He was probably appalled, but he merely sat in his corner, watching. After all, there was an explanation for all this decadence: it was part of the students' English language tuition.

Even though the government cracked down on the Democracy Wall movement, political experiments with democracy continued. Indeed, Beida in 1980 would conduct student elections. I was fascinated by the process, mostly because the Philippines has a political culture like no other place—part fiesta, part blood feud, part cockfight, part morality play. Getting out to vote in the Philippines often involves money and violence. But Filipinos love politics and the exercise of voting is essential to our character as political animals. How would my classmates in Beida take to elections?

In 1979, China's legislature, the National People's Congress (NPC), approved a new law that called for the election of deputies to county and district legislatures. These local congresses were to serve as the base of a pyramid of increasingly larger people's congresses, with the NPC at the top. For the first time in over thirty years, direct elections were to be held nationwide. The law stipulated that a minimum of three voters could nominate a candidate. Groups of electors were then allowed to campaign.

At Beida, eighteen students ran for two seats on the Haidian district People's Congress. And in late 1980, these candidates and their supporters put up wall posters outlining their programs and platforms. One of the first to declare candidacy was Zhang Wei, an economics major of the Class of '77 and a friend of mine. Soft-spoken yet politically savvy, Zhang was already a popular campus figure and the president of Beida's Student Union, which he had won by indirect election, picked by representatives of the university's departments. He was a respected member of the Communist Party and appeared to be on the ladder for success, lined up for a senior role in the Communist Youth League.

Zhang was as well-versed in Western economic theory as he was in Marxist politics. He stood for a moderate approach to reform. He was critical of past radical politics but, while extolling democracy, stopped short of rejecting the existing structure of political power. Instead, he advocated modulated reform, with improvements coming a step at a time. In his declaration of candidacy, he wrote: "Democratization is an objective progression that takes place regardless of one's will. We should put forward practical demands and solutions according to our country's actual conditions. Otherwise, we will not get the democratic rights that we deserve, and we will create chaos and regression." He had a keen awareness of what was happening. I thought it was a cinch that he'd win a seat. I even imagined that one day he might be China's premier.

There were other notable candidates. One of the boldest and wittiest was Hu Ping, a 33-year-old graduate student in philosophy, who advocated setting up institutionalized checks-and-balances, a reform that would most certainly threaten the centrality of the Communist Party. Hu would drop exotic-sounding names—like Hegel, Kant and J.S. Mill—to impress the voters he was trying to win over. The one thing he always mentioned was "freedom of speech."

"I talked about other issues, but I always highlighted this theme," Hu recalled. "I thought if I could make people remember that point after speaking in an event, then that was good enough."

There were some candidates who advocated radical changes. Among them was Wang Juntao, a physics major with a reputation as a firebrand. Only twenty-two when I met him, Wang was already an alternate member of the Communist Youth League's central committee when he enrolled in Beida, traditionally a step in grooming those destined for prominent political careers. He was fiery and had gotten into trouble with the authorities before, including being jailed for taking part in the April 5th Movement in 1976, the spontaneous mass protest against the so-called "Gang of Four" that rose out of mourning for the late premier Zhou Enlai. Wang's campaign manifesto in Beida was: "Let us, the new generation, push China forward!"

Then there was Zhang Manling, a young woman in the Chinese literature department. She had become a Beida celebrity because of her distinctive look: Almost elfin, she often wore a custom-made leather hat over a buzz-cut. A native of southwestern Yunnan province, she pressed for women's rights and feminist ideals, which she tried to crystalize in the slogan "*nüxing mei*" (feminine beauty) as a path to "realize the value of human beings." At a time when most students still strove to be *guai haizi* — well-behaved children — she was in-your-face and unafraid of being controversial. Indeed, she was also among those detained after the large public gathering to mourn Premier Zhou in April 1976 turned into a protest.

Yang Baikui, a student in the International Relations Department, chose to become a candidate, he later told me, because he thought that politics was fun. "Aside from doing class work, I discussed politics and exchanged underground publications with classmates. That's why I decided to run." During the two-month campaign period, Yang and his supporters put up posters detailing his biography and his ideas, including the limitations and flaws of totalitarianism. "We talked about Mao Zedong and the Cultural Revolution. We also talked about women's issues, gender equality, family values."

None of the candidates spent much money on their campaigns. Said Hu, "Paper, brushes and ink were all provided by the school and the sound system was free of charge, too." A dozen of his classmates volunteered to do the legwork. "There were no typewriters, no photocopiers," Yang said. "We had to handprint big-character posters, mimeograph handouts and distribute them ourselves."

Campaigning climaxed in big town-hall meetings held in the cafeterias and auditoriums, with candidates debating each other. These were followed by question-and-answer sessions with the audience. Everything from the meaning of democracy to Deng's market-oriented reforms was the subject of open and hot argumentation. Some in the audiences, of course, were more interested in immediate and practical campus issues. One person said the cafeteria needed to serve better food. Another complained about over-crowding in dormitories. Still another demanded a stronger student voice in determining university policies.

Early into the campaign period, the Beijing city government became jittery about the campus elections and tried to stop them. But the Beida administration resisted the government pressure and allowed them to proceed. "It was the only successful democratic grassroots election that ever happened in China since the 1950s," said Bai Weiji, a classmate of mine in the history department and a political junkie with an encyclopedic knowledge of party machinations. "The students adopted Western rules and procedures that they learned from textbooks and news reports, and school authorities respected the students' political rights granted by the constitution. Such activities could not have taken place if Beida were against them."

On the day of the elections students, teachers and employees on campus cast their secret ballots in makeshift counters set up in the main cafeteria. Voters' turnout was an impressive 91.2%. Hu Ping topped the tally, getting 3,467 votes out of the 6,084 total votes, followed by Wang Juntao with 2,964 votes and Zhang Wei with 2,052. Zhang Manling picked up 695 votes. My former roommate Jiang Wenran, who did not campaign, received about 100 write-in votes, which the election rules allowed. While two district congress slots were up for grabs, Hu Ping was considered a winner because he was the only candidate who received 50% or more of the total votes cast, again as the rules stipulated. But he never got to take up his seat.

The 1980 elections in Beida were inspired by Deng's "liberation of the mind" speech in late 1978. However, the elections unintentionally put the ruling party's record under scrutiny. As students debated the burning issues, they learned about the "mistakes" of Mao and the shortcomings of the political system. Some students went further by probing the meaning of liberal democracy and flirted with political and economic concepts that were borrowed from Western countries. In the end, the student activists breached the limits of Deng's tolerance. There would be no district deputies elected to fill local congresses anywhere—not at Beida or Haidian, nor in any county in the country.

The fact that this one university pressed on with the vote despite opposition from the authorities inspired many students. "The 1980 elections left a deep impression on me," Hu would tell me years later. "Before that, I did not feel much affection for Beida. After the elections, I felt that Beida was my Beida."

10

NEW LIVES

THE PARCHMENT of my Beida diploma isn't what it used to be. My father, proud that his son had finally graduated from college, had it embellished with a blue banner declaring "Peking University" in English; he also added translations so visitors could understand the certificate when they saw it on the wall in his home in the Philippines, where he displayed it for all to see. But the original can still be made out: my name is in Chinese calligraphy, the characters are a transliteration: "ji-mi fu-luo-ke-lu-zi." The round red circle of the Beida seal—a Chinese style official "chop"—is stamped over the name of the school's president Zhang Longxiang. At the bottom left is the official diploma number "82004," issued on March 1, 1982.

The graduation ceremony itself was in keeping with the spirit and style of the first four-year class to emerge from the Cultural Revolution. There was little pomp and ceremony. In fact, there was no ceremony at all. Students, parents, and teachers did not gather in any sort of convocation, as they do in the rest of the world and in China nowadays. Even Chinese high schools today celebrate graduation with much more warmth and a sense of accomplishment.

We assembled for a group photograph in front of the building where most of our classes had been held. We wore Mao jackets in one of three hues: green, blue, or gray. Today, the graduates of Beida wear Western-style graduation gowns and throw their caps into the air at the end of the ceremony. No such thing back then. No one was called on stage to pick up their diplomas and pose for photographs with the Dean. Yet we all suspected that we were special. We would never be called the class of 1982, even though that was the year we graduated. We would always be the Class of '77, the first survivors of the ideological maelstrom, the first of the *beidaren* (people of Beida, or alumni) to be educated to bring China into modernity, which has long been the core quest of Beida.

So, a month before graduation, many of us began to create mementoes, going around with notebooks or albums asking our friends, classmates, and teachers to write down how we could stay in touch, asking for even a little note to remember them by. Most people responded by writing fond little notes of a personal nature. But you could tell which graduates were thinking big. Li Keqiang, who would eventually become prime minister of China, wrote in one classmate's album: "Broaden your horizons."

My classmate Lu Danni says that one teacher, intent on ideological rectitude, wrote on her album, "Strive to join the Chinese Communist Party soon!" (Lu has yet to join, more than thirty years after graduation.) A few students who had formed a study group issued an essay bidding farewell to the school on behalf of the Class of '77, saying, "It's hard to part from the weeping willows on the banks of the Weiming Lake."

But generally, sentimentality was at a minimum. Lu Danni, who was in the history department with me, recalls collecting donations for upright and worthy causes, specifically for the erection of monuments to the memory of Cai Yuanpei and Li Dazhao, two of the founders of Beida. Each student gave the equivalent of $1, no small amount at the time. And the closest thing we did to a graduation ceremony was a formal meeting of representatives of the Class of '77 not on campus, but at the Great Hall of the People next to Tiananmen Square. The choice of venue was a reminder that the students were to remain loyal to the Communist Party as they served China. The main speaker at the event was Bo Yibo, who was then the Vice Chairman of the Central Advisory Commission, one of the most important agencies set up by Deng Xiaoping upon his return to power. Bo was one of the great survivors of the Cultural Revolution: he had been imprisoned and beaten, and his sons, too, were imprisoned. One of them was Bo Xilai, a fellow member of the Class of '77.

Graduation was also a test in many ways. Finishing at Beida meant I would no longer have a legal reason to reside in China. I needed fulltime a job. It also meant I needed to find a new place to live. The dorms were no longer going to be available to me.

Fortunately, my friend Huang Lanyou, a physicist educated in the U.S. and Germany, had a spacious apartment provided by the Chinese Academy of Sciences, and it was about to become even more spacious. His wife Zhang Weihua, a concert pianist, was set to go to the U.S. for post-graduate training, and his teenage daughter Huang Wei had just graduated high school and was about to attend an American college. The family decided to send his son Huang Yong, in his early teens, to Nanjing and live with his grandparents while attending high school there.

I packed up my books into a big box and put my clothes and other belongings into the hard-case luggage I had brought with me from the Philippines more than ten years earlier. The suitcase looked much the same except that the handle had broken and fallen off and I had replaced it with a thick piece of rope.

By then, most of my classmates who were from outside the capital had gone home. But about ten of us remained and gathered at a restaurant near the university. We brought parting gifts to exchange and promised to stay in touch. The camaraderie brought tears to my eyes. I had plans and dreams, just like them. We were all off on the great adventure of remaking China — with much drama and heartbreak to come.

China in the second decade of the 21st Century is a spectacular success. As an economic engine, it was not only the factory of the world but contributed tremendously to the global growth. Much of the intellectual and political power that made that possible emanated from the graduates of Beida. In terms of material success alone, according to a 2015 survey, thirty-five graduates of Beida — not just of the Class of '77 — had an estimated net worth of $1.4 billion. Among them were Robin Li Yanhong, (a 1991 physics graduate), CEO of Baidu.com; Wang Zhidong (a 1988 radio electronics graduate), the former CEO of Sina.com; and Yu Minhong, (a 1985 English language graduate), founder and president of New Oriental Education and Technology Group.

Beida has also produced its share of financial miscreants. Wang Yi, Class of '77 archeology graduate, has been languishing in jail since 2008, after he was convicted of alleged insider trading, bribery and womanizing. He had risen to the heights of vice-chairman of the China Development Bank, an institution that funded many of the country's immense and expensive infrastructure projects. At one point, the CDB had outstanding loans that rivaled that of the World Bank. He had served in that position for over nine years. Before that, Wang was vice chairman of the China Securities Regulatory Commission, the chief regulator of the country's financial industry, and deputy director of the securities office for the State Council, China's cabinet. Like many of our classmates, he was gifted in many ways. A self-taught musician, Wang composed the well-received and popular "Ode to China," a contemporary classical symphony performed by prominent Chinese and foreign orchestras in China and overseas. He was accused of taking $1.8 billion in bribes and was given a suspended death sentence.

Beida is proud to be the producer of billionaires, but its graduates have also gone on to success in other areas. Zha Jianying, of the Class of '77, is one of the most successful journalists to emerge from Mainland China, writing in both English and Chinese. She is the author of the *Tide Players* and *China Pop*, chronicles of the transformation of China since the reforms of Deng Xiaoping. The daughter of a professor at the Chinese Academy of Social Sciences, she and her family suffered political persecution and public humiliation, like most members of their class, during the Cultural Revolution. She was eighteen and laboring in a farm when China restored the *gaokao*. Passing it, she says, "was like waking up from a dream."

"I came directly from the farm and looked like a real country bumpkin," she recalled. "I wore old clothes and looked so skinny and tanned that my classmates thought I was a farmer." Still, she thrived in Beida, contributing to an underground literary magazine, apart from the official publication of the literature department. "We shared a spirit of independence and inquiry, a feeling of being on our own. There was a free-spirit attitude, which was equally important." She now divides her time between New York and Beijing and is a regular contributor for *The New Yorker* magazine.

In 1977, Beida was the first university in China to reboot its law department. The profession had been abolished as a tool of capitalism when the Cultural Revolution began in 1966. Liu Fengming, a busboy in a state-run restaurant in Lanzhou, capital of his home province of Gansu, passed the *gaokao* and decided to enter Beida's law school. He says his parents "did not believe me until I showed them my admission notice. It was a big deal because only six applicants from the entire Gansu province got into Beida that year."

It was an important thing to be among the first lawyers to go into business in 1982. "We were able to fill many important vacancies, working in the judiciary, teaching in colleges, doing research, or working in the government. Because there were no college graduates during the previous ten years, we enjoyed unprecedented opportunities." Liu himself ended up being hired to work as in-house counsel for a number of multinational companies. But the most successful member of Beida's law department was Li Keqiang, China's premier.

Among the more prominent of the Class of 1977 is the economist Yi Gang. After Beida, he went to the United States for post-graduate work and eventually got a Ph.D in Economics from the University of Illinois. He became an associate professor with tenure at the Indiana University-Purdue and then joined the Beida faculty as professor. In 1997, Yi moved to the People's Bank of China (PBOC), the country's central bank. When I interviewed him in the fall of 2000, he told me that he was one of about a dozen overseas-trained Chinese technocrats—lawyers, doctors, accountants working in the U.S. and Europe—who were enticed back home by then Premier Zhu Rongji. Zhu was keen to shake things up in the bureaucracy and in the world of Chinese business to push forward stalled reforms. Modest and low-key, just as I remembered him from our college days, Yi also sounded excited that he was involved in changing China and appeared determined to bring in the ideas he had acquired overseas. "Most things are already set and settled in the U.S.," he remarked. "Here we are just drawing things up."

Yi has thrived in China's nascent financial sector. Previously, from 2007 he had served as a PBOC deputy governor and Director of the State Administration of Foreign Exchange (SAFE). Because of his familiarity with global affairs and fluency in English, Yi has frequently represented China overseas and has been a familiar presence in forums like the World Economic Forum in Davos. In 2018, he was promoted as Governor of the PBOC, roughly the equivalent of the U.S, Federal Reserve, making him one of the most influential of China's financial policy makers.

Zhao Leji, a Class of '77 philosophy major, in 2017 earned his seat at the seven-member Standing Committee of the Politburo, the elite policy-making body of the Communist Party and now manages the party's Organization Department. In that position, he vets and helps decide on personnel appointments, dismissals, and promotions of cadres and senior officials across China. In effect, Zhao is the Communist Party's human resources manager and is able to place Xi Jinping's party loyalists in strategic posts.

Another one of the up-and-coming political figures in China today is from Beida, but not the Class of '77. Still, he's close. Hu Chunhua, born April 1963, topped the *gaokao* in his home county to enter the university in 1979—at the age of sixteen—and, since November 2012, has become one of the youngest members of the Communist Party's politburo.

Hu was born to a family of farmers in Hubei province. He majored in Chinese language and literature and, after graduation, volunteered to work for the Communist Youth League in Tibet, designated as an enclave for an ethnic minority living in the Himalayan mountains. It was a difficult assignment but potentially a valuable one if one did well. There, he rose through the ranks. He has been called "little Hu" due to the similarities of his career to that of Hu Jintao (no relation), China's state president from 2002 to 2012. Hu Jintao, too, had been given difficult assignments, including top posts in the impoverished provinces of Guizhou and Tibet, before rising to the Number One position in the People's Republic.

In 2012, after serving as governor of two other provinces, Hu Chunhua was appointed Party Secretary of Guangdong, the progressive southern province that borders Hong Kong. In summer of 2017, several days before Guangzhou hosted the Fortune Global Forum, he met a group of us, U.S.-based organizers of the business conference that would fly in CEOs of Fortune 500 companies. It was the third time a Chinese city was to host the prestigious gathering of global business and political leaders. The first took place in 1999 in Shanghai, powerbase of the former president Jiang Zemin. This time, the spotlight had turned to Guangzhou, Guangdong's provincial capital and an emerging hub of global trade and innovation.

Speaking softly, Hu ticked off policy talking points laced with statistics as he gave a tour d'horizon of Guangdong's ambition to become a hub of innovation. The Beida alumnus struck me more like a policy wonk than a party apparatchik ruling over of one of China's most prosperous provinces.

Hu Chunhua is considered one of the under-studies to become China's next premier when his fellow Beida alumnus Li Keqiang steps down. He has formidable rivals but his relative youth and rich experience makes him one of the front-runners. Hu has maintained a relatively low public profile during his rise to higher positions of power. In 2018, he was promoted as one of four vice-premiers and currently sits on the 25-member Politburo, the decision-making body that is one notch below its seven-member Standing Committee.

But several graduates have become antagonistic to the regime's policies. Among them is Hu Ping, who won the 1980 district elections in Haidian that Beida conducted. Born in Beijing in 1947, Hu Ping grew up in Chengdu, the capital city of Sichuan, where his family moved when he was eight. He finished high school there in 1966, just when the ten-year Cultural Revolution started. He showed great courage during the upheaval, self-publishing a newsletter reprinting the essays of Yu Luoke, a young liberal dissident who was executed as the Red Guard swept through China. Yu was attacked by the radical Maoists.

Entering Beida after taking the 1978 *gaokao*, Hu Ping took an active part in the 1979 Democracy Wall movement, posting "*dazibao*" (big-character posters) on the famous brick wall on Beijing's main drag. He also gave impromptu speeches in front of hundreds of people who gathered at the wall during the days of political ferment. When the government refused to seat some of the winners of the 1980 elections, Hu Ping was one of them. Increasingly disaffected, Hu went to the United States for post-graduate studies in 1987. He would move fully into dissidence there, becoming chairman of the China Democratic Federation in 1988 and editing anti-regime magazines like "China Spring" and "Beijing Spring," advocating freedom of speech and democracy. Unable to go back to China because of his views, Hu nevertheless remembers his years at Beida fondly. "I believe it is not easy to find another institution in the whole country like Beida," he told me. "Living overseas, I feel a close affinity whenever I meet fellow Beida alumni, even on first meeting. I am deeply proud as a Beidaren."

And what did I do after graduation? I had wanted to become a journalist ever since I learned the rudiments of the craft at my high school newspaper in the Philippines. I worked as a cub reporter in college and later editor-in-chief of our college paper. I was elected chairman of a national college editors association months before I left for China in 1971. Getting stuck in China derailed my career, but when I was a rising senior in Beida, I got another chance. After 1979, American media companies started setting up shop in China as ties between Beijing and Washington warmed up. Many were looking for English-speaking local freelancers — stringers — to work for their budding operations.

Among those who had found a freelance gig was Jan Wong, a Canadian of Chinese descent who later wrote a best-selling book *Red China Blues*. Over dinner in summer of 1981, she talked excitedly about how she had been working as research assistant for Fox Butterfield, The New York Times' newly arrived correspondent. She knew other correspondents who were also looking to hire part-time research assistants.

Jan said I should apply too, so the next day I knocked on the doors of *Newsweek* and the *Baltimore Sun*. I was offered about $400 a month, a lot of money in China at that time. But I was worried. What would my Chinese mentors and benefactors, who were responsible for my behavior, think if I were to work for what Chinese conservative critics disparage as "a propaganda tool of American imperialism"?

I turned to Teacher Cai Huosheng, a balding party member and one of my Beida "minders" who worked for the Foreign Students' Office. I told him of my predicament. I said I was interested in the job because I had always wanted to be a journalist, and wished to earn my keep, become self-reliant to lighten the burden I imposed on my Chinese hosts. I wondered aloud: should I take up the job, which I greatly desired?

"Jimi," Teacher Cai intoned, looking at me in the eye through his black-rimmed glasses. "You've lived in China for ten years. You're a mature and grown man. You know the right thing to do."

Then he left me to ponder what he meant. Was that a "yes" or a "no"? I sensed in my gut that it was a "yes". Otherwise, he would have summarily said, "No way." The only way to find out was to do it. In the subsequent days, weeks, and months, after I'm done with class, I would take a taxi to work at *Newsweek's* newly minted Beijing bureau temporarily located in Qianmen

Hotel, just south of Tiananmen Square. I did not hear about it again from Teacher Cai. I worked there for about a year and a half.

Initially my job was to read Chinese and foreign publications that *Newsweek* subscribed to and then clip and file selected stories. But when bureau chief Melinda Liu realized that I spoke Chinese and had many Chinese friends, she decided to give the clipping and filing job to others and encouraged me to do field reporting. That gave me a chance to pitch and write my own stories. My big break came a few months later when I reported on the December 1981–January 1982 trial of Chairman Mao's widow, Jiang Qing, and the "Gang of Four." For two consecutive weeks, *Newsweek's* stories on the trial had my tiny byline tucked in at the bottom of the piece. I had become a published journalist.

In the spring of 1982, when I graduated from Beida, I needed a full-time job in order to be accredited as an official China-based correspondent. Otherwise, I might not be able to continue to stay in China, because I was no longer a student at Beida and I still had no passport. And then I might have become a completely homeless citizen of the world. Without an official accreditation I could not get access to housing and other benefits of residency.

I also couldn't get a Chinese passport. I have lived in China for nearly 50 years, but even if I lived here for a hundred years, I still would not be eligible for Chinese citizenship because China follows the *jus saguinis,* or right relating to blood. Yes, there were some exceptional cases many decades ago when a few expatriates — mostly foreigners who had supported the Chinese Communist cause — were given Chinese citizenship. But I was, and always will be, an expatriate in China, and I wanted to proudly wave the Philippine flag.

In the meantime, I had moved into my friend Huang's apartment, made spacious by his wife and kids' departure. His residence was a good one-hour bike ride to Newsweek's office in downtown Beijing so I invested in a second-hand car. It was a white Toyota that I bought from a Brazilian diplomat who was ending his China posting. It was a luxury, but it became essential to my career. Much more essential was getting a job in journalism that would get me my accreditation. I asked Newsweek if I could stay as a full-fledged reporter but was told I had to wait for about six months when a new bureau chief was expected. Only then could they decide on it.

So I knocked on the door of Newsweek's great rival, TIME. The magazine's Beijing bureau chief Richard Bernstein, an old China hand, already knew me and my work. He promptly offered to hire me as a full-time reporter. Months later, TIME formally applied for my press credentials as the magazine's second reporter in China. In 1982, I joined TIME magazine as reporter. It was the beginning of a long and satisfying career, something I would never have predicted when I first took the train into China from Hong Kong back in August 1971. I was with the magazine for almost two decades, working my way up to become TIME's Beijing bureau chief from 1990 to 2000. I took a year's sabbatical as the 2001 Edward R. Murrow Press Fellow at the Council of Foreign Relations in New York. And after that I became the Beijing bureau chief for CNN until my retirement in 2015.

In the middle of all this, I was finally able to visit the Philippines for the first time in twelve years. I would also find the love of my life there.

11

EVERYTHING CHANGES

WHEN OUR GROUP of fifteen crossed into China from Hong Kong in August 1971, relations between the Philippines and the People's Republic were dismal. In March of the same year, six young Filipinos had hijacked a Philippine Airlines jet that had taken off from Manila, bound for southern Davao, and forced it to fly first to Hong Kong and then to Guangzhou. Asked by the Chinese officials why they hijacked the plane to China, they said they wanted to learn from the Chinese Revolution, learn guerrilla warfare and return to the Philippines to start a revolution, a la Che Guevarra. The Chinese were amused, one of the hijackers recalled.

With a Maoist insurgency raging in the Philippine countryside, President Ferdinand Marcos did not look kindly on even more Filipinos heading into China to learn from its revolutionary peasantry. Two years after I arrived in China, he imposed Martial Law on the country, mainly he said to combat the threat of the communist-led New People's Army. It was also intended to snuff out the legal opposition that was set to sweep the election later that year.

But ties were bound to improve. Richard Nixon's February 1972 historic trip to China provided political impetus to America's allies in Asia to establish ties with the mainland. The very next month, Salvador Laurel Jr., a Philippine senator, visited Beijing on official business and inquired after the conditions not only of the hijackers but of the rest of us. The Chinese diplomatically said that everyone was in good condition and "working in communes." In his report to the Philippine Senate, Laurel cited Beijing's explanation: "They are homesick but afraid to come home because they face arrest on charges of violating the Anti-Subversion Law."

In 1974, Marcos's flamboyant wife Imelda made her own historic trip to Beijing and apparently charmed both Mao and his wife Jiang Qing. At that point, the Philippines still recognized the Nationalist government based in Taiwan as the legitimate government of all of China. That changed the next year, when Manila declared formal normalization of relations with Beijing (the U.S. had established a diplomatic liaison office in Beijing in 1973 but would not formally switch recognition till 1979). Filipino diplomats would soon start living in Beijing. But, given my political history, I did not want to risk walking into the Philippine Embassy — technically Filipino territory — and be whisked back to my homeland and face an unimaginable fate.

That changed as Filipino diplomats themselves started reaching out — and made sincere attempts at reconciliation. In particular, the embassy's cultural officer (and later Consul General), Nona Zaldivar, kept a motherly eye on Filipino scholars in China — including me. She often hosted Filipino students and teachers from Beida and the Beijing Languages Institute for a home-cooked meal or an overnight stay in her living room. Nona and I became good friends. We shared a keen interest in Chinese history and culture and personal views on the goings-on in the Philippines. She knew how homesick I was — and she was going to do something about it.

Sometime in the middle of 1981, she introduced me to the

new Philippine ambassador to China, Fortunato Abat, a retired army general close to the Marcos family. One of his sons – also a soldier in the Philippine military – had been killed in 1979 in a clash with Maoist guerrillas. Would he really help a former leftist student exile? I'd had an application for a new passport waiting in limbo for five years and had almost given up all hope for it.

But the ambassador and I became friends. An avuncular retired soldier, Abat did not allow our political differences to stand in the way. He often invited me to the embassy to play badminton, his favorite sport. One day, in June 1983, Nona called me into the embassy and handed me a newly minted passport, which she had signed. I was later told that when the Presidential Palace in Manila phoned Abat to ask for his advice on my passport application – which had somehow gotten attention – he said something like, "Oh, Jimi is a good man, he often comes to the embassy to visit me." That was enough for Marcos' office to greenlight the document for me. And my exile was over. It was legal for me to return to the Philippines.

I started to make plans to go home for a visit. But the second half of 1983 proved to be a cataclysmic one in the Philippines. On August 21, the very same day I first arrived in China twelve years earlier, the popular opposition leader Benigno Aquino Jr. was assassinated upon disembarking from his plane in Manila. Aquino was on a trip home from political exile in the United States. Imelda Marcos herself had warned him against returning home, saying she could not guarantee his safety. The country was plunged into turmoil as huge segments of the country immediately suspected Marcos as the mastermind of the killing.

Although I was carrying a newly minted Philippine passport, I had to postpone my homecoming. It's not safe to return, my family and friends advised. But I was itching to travel out of the Middle Kingdom. What is the outside world like, twelve years into my China exile? I was keen to find out. Since it was not advisable to fly home, I decided to visit Hong Kong and Tokyo, where friends and friends of friends were happy to host my stay or at least hold my hand.

I was very anxious when I first took a flight out of China. Where should I stay? How do I get there? How much money do I need to carry with me? How much should I tip the taxi drivers? I was worrying over those trivial questions as I fastened my seatbelt on a CAAC flight from Beijing to Hong Kong. Then I noticed two fellow passengers sitting next to me. They looked like they were in the early fifties and had identical shirts and haircuts. It seemed they had never flown before because I saw them fumbling with their seat belts. They did not know how to clasp together the two ends of the seat belt. I proudly showed them how to do it and heaved a sigh of relief. At least I knew that.

As I was walking through immigration, I saw Nancy Berliner, an American student at the China Academy of Fine Arts who was on the same flight. We chatted, and I told her I needed to make a phone call to a friend's friend who had kindly agreed to pick me up at the airport and put me up in his Hong Kong home. Nancy pointed out to me the line of telephones that the airport, at that time, Kai Tak Airport, had available for free use for people just arriving. Delighted, I ran over to use one. It turned out to be a bit unfamiliar. I looked and looked but could not find the dial. I hung up and walked over to Nancy. It must be a *neibu* (for internal use) phone, I told her, just like in China; they have no dials. Amused, she explained that this is a new style phone with the dials fastened on the receiver. I laughed because I felt like the two Chinese travelers who did not know how to fasten the seat belt ends together.

Hong Kong was the wrong destination to visit for someone

who had just spent twelve years in a hermit land. I was impressed watching the neatly dressed throngs of commuters walking briskly to work. I was even more dazzled by the glass-and-steel skyscrapers that dotted the city's skyline. As I strolled the streets, I noticed that I was instinctively looking upwards, just like what a provincial in China would do while visiting Shanghai for the first time.

Whenever I walked into the malls and emporiums, I felt overwhelmed by the range and volume of goods available. Choices galore, I remember thinking. The first time I went shopping, I left the malls empty-handed because I could not decide what to buy. I walked into a restaurant for a quick meal.

"A sandwich, please," I said.

"Sure, what kind of bread would you like—white bread, whole-wheat, rye or croissant?"

"Ah, just get me a simple salad instead."

"Sure, but what kind of dressing would you prefer—French, Caesar, Thousand Island, or vinaigrette?"

Choices, choices, choices. Decisions, decisions. I had no clue.

For one brief moment, I yearned for the bad old China days, when I was served a fistful of steamed buns and a pile of pickled radish, take it or leave it. Simple living and hard struggle, Chairman Mao called it aptly. I recall the days when I would walk into the Dongfeng (East Wind) Department Store, the biggest in central Beijing. The poorly lit five-story building was stocked with a range of proletarian essentials branded with distinctive names: "Peony" radios, "Wild Flower" shoes, "Green Bamboo" toilet paper, "Red Lantern" toothpaste, "Evergreen" canned foods, "Shaolin" plasters and "Golden Harvest" pumps. Even in the late 1970s, when Deng's reform had already started and daily life was beginning to look up, one simple source of bliss for me was sitting with friends in the lobby of Peking

Hotel, gulping down cold Yanjing beer, as we watched Beijing's expatriate community walk by.

It was December 1983 when I got back home for the first time in more than a dozen years. The mood in Manila remained tense, but my family advised that it was now okay to return as long as I kept a low profile. Besides, my cousin Jorge had made "special arrangements" through his network of "connections". To ensure my safety, Jorge and my uncle Luis FlorCruz would pick me up at the airport accompanied by a pair of soldiers in civilian clothes who had connections in the airport.

My plane landed at the Manila International Airport only several minutes late. I unfastened my seat belt and cautiously followed a few passengers to disembark. As I walked past the "tube" connecting the plane to the terminal, I instinctively turned around once or twice, rewinding in my mind the video clip of how uniformed soldiers fatally shot Senator Benigno Aquino from behind while he disembarked from a plane in the same airport just four months earlier. Several steps in front of the immigration area, I saw Jorge and my uncle, waving. After quick hugs, one man walked up and took my passport while another ushered us past the immigration counter—no questions asked—straight to the luggage claim area. Minutes later, the contact-man handed back my passport duly stamped with an entry seal. I never learned how much money passed hands for that "VIP reception".

That's the Philippines I returned to after twelve years. Politics was everywhere in the turbulent aftermath of the Aquino murder. Many problems—poor-rich divide, corruption, repression—issues that I raged against twelve years earlier remained unsolved. But I was sensitive to the fact that I owed my passport to my friendship with a Marcos ally—and did not want to embarrass him or endanger my own ability to stay in the

Philippines by engaging in politics, even though I had a visceral hatred for the president. And so I kept a low profile. I spent most of the time at home with my family and close friends. I had a most joyful Christmas that year, finally reunited with my parents and most siblings. My brother Rene and family were also back home on vacation from the U.S.

As advised, I steered away from big gatherings and mass meetings. I did make a few exceptions, like the pre-Christmas reunion hosted by Sheila Coronel, an intrepid investigative reporter who later moved to Columbia University in New York as professor and director of its Stabile Center for Investigative Journalism. The dinner party brought together scores of old friends and college contemporaries, including journalists, writers, professors, and human rights lawyers. Many of them were in the frontline of the smoldering opposition against the Marcos dictatorship.

Among them were members of Women Writers In Media Now, a group of feisty women journalists, including Jo-Ann Maglipon, my girlfriend before I left Manila for Beijing 12 years earlier. By this time, Jo-Ann had settled down, happily married to a college contemporary. In 1974, two years after joining the underground resistance against Marcos' martial law rule, she was arrested, tortured and jailed for one year. She remained a fearless writer, raging against government corruption and repression. Conversations with Jo-Ann and the other guests convinced me that the days of the Marcos regime were numbered.

Several days after Christmas holidays, an old friend, a local journalist, was showing me around the city when we came across a picket line. Scores of students, actors and filmmakers were protesting outside the home of the chairwoman of the country's board of censors. They were angry over its decision to ban a movie. I kept my distance and watched from the sidelines.

Among the gaggle of kibitzers, it turned out, were Nona's sister Lorna and her husband Raul Segovia, whom I had visited in their home days earlier. Lorna tugged at me and pointed to a long-haired figure in the picket line walking in circles, carrying placards and yelling slogans against state censorship.

"That's my daughter Ana," she said proudly.

I would not forget the face. It would take more than a year, but I was destined to meet her. In China.

I'd had my heart broken twice, by Hai Ou and by Wenjing. I didn't stop seeing women or having a fling here and there. But no serious romances, certainly not with Chinese nationals. I'd date *huayi* women—foreign nationals of Chinese ancestry –as well as other expats who shared my interests in China and things Chinese. I had serious relationships, but I didn't see my life as a bachelor changing. Until I met Ana again.

It was the summer of 1985, and I'd been invited to a lunch get-together at the residence of Agnes Prieto, the press officer of the Philippine Embassy. Her apartment was on the ground floor of a building next to the TIME magazine office in the Qijiayuan Diplomatic Compound, about a ten-minute cab ride from Tiananmen Square. It wasn't a long trip for me: I had a sublet studio in another building in the same compound—small, but it was impossible to move up to a larger one because of the Chinese bureaucracy. It almost made getting a passport seem easy.

I walked into Agnes' apartment just a few minutes late. There were about a dozen people gathered in the living room, including Nona. And there was her niece, Ana Segovia. She introduced us. Ana had just graduated from the University of the Philippines and was visiting her aunt. It was her first trip to China. I nodded and said, "Yes, I've seen you before." That intrigued her but the lunch party got underway and I didn't have a chance to explain. We were seated farthest away from each other at Agnes' long dinner table.

With lunch over, I had to go back to work. But, back at the TIME bureau, I spent the rest of the afternoon plotting how to see Ana again. I had one idea.

Right after work, I drove two blocks to the Jianguomenwai Diplomatic Compound where Nona had her apartment. I'd visited several times before because she'd always made expat Filipinos feel at home there.

When Nona answered the door, I told her that today was the big soccer match between China and Hong Kong at Beijing's Workers Stadium. "My TV's broken," I fibbed. "May I watch the soccer match here?"

"Sure," Nona smiled and let me in. She apologized that she could not stay because she was about to leave for the Beijing Capital Airport to meet a delegation from the Philippines. She said Ana was around and would keep me company. I did not complain.

For the rest of the evening, Ana and I talked, while occasionally glancing at the soccer match on TV. I was completely taken by how beautiful she was. She spoke sparingly and listened intently. And more importantly, it was very clear she was weighing everything I had to say — and judging whether it was smart or not.

She had just been accepted into the College of Law at the University of the Philippines, after passing competitive entrance exams and a round with a panel of harsh law school interviewers. It was one of the toughest law schools to get into. She was scheduled to start her courses after the summer break. Law was part of her family legacy. Her maternal grandfather, Calixto O. Zaldivar, a prominent lawyer and political leader at home, capped his career as an associate justice of the Philippine Supreme Court. In 1972, he was the only member of the highest court to dissent when it endorsed President Marcos' decision to rule by decree.

Ana said she was lukewarm about the idea of going back to school. After all the schoolwork, she claimed she needed to get over burnout. To my alarm, she said she planned to stay in China only for a month. I knew I must "seize the day; seize the hour," recalling lines from Chairman Mao's Little Red Book. And so, I told her about when I had seen her in Manila in 1984, how her mother pointed her out in the picket line. And how I'd never forgotten her since that fleeting moment.

She'd just arrived the previous day and had not seen much of Beijing. I asked if she would join me for lunch the following day. She said yes.

"Do you know how to ride a bicycle?" I asked.

She hesitated for a second, and then said yes. She would borrow Nona's bike. I was going to work very hard to impress her and planned out the itinerary carefully.

And so, on our first date, we pedaled down expansive Chang'an Avenue and I tried to impress Ana with my knowledge of Beijing, its history and geography. I pointed out the top of an antique tower and explained that it contained a sundial and other astronomical instruments introduced by the Jesuits from Europe during the Ming Dynasty.

"The tower's what's left of the old Ming-era city wall," I added. I pointed at the opposite direction. "That's the Second Ring Road, Beijing's main artery which goes around the city."

Beijing used to have an ancient city wall, about 500 years old, which encircled the city, but in the late 1960s, it was torn down to make way for the highway and a metro line, and to provide bricks to build air raid shelters. "It's a shame they failed to keep the city wall."

On and on I went: how Beijing boasted of layers of defenses

to keep invaders away, how the city is still dotted by gates and watch towers, which delineated the Outer City, the Inner City and the Imperial City, where the emperor and his retinue used to live.

To further impress her, I took her on a tour of the Peking Hotel, which was built in 1917 and the most prestigious in the capital. It had been renovated and expanded a number of times since, as it played host to important visitors from overseas. Our first stop was Block C, a red-brick high-rise built in 1954.

"I stayed here with my visiting group when we first arrived in August 1971," I said matter-of-factly. "Up in the top floor rooms, you get a commanding view of the Forbidden City and part of the Tiananmen Square." (Indeed, it would be from a balcony on an upper floor of an adjacent section of the hotel that the famous photograph of "tank man" was taken on June 5, two days after the military had suppressed the demonstrations that had taken over the Square.)

I showed her the main banquet hall where Chairman Mao and other communist leaders used to go ballroom dancing in the 1950s and '60s. I walked her past grand facades and elegant corridors before we finally turned left into what was simply known as the *Dongdating*—the East Wing Grand Hall. And there was our destination: the best Sichuan food in town.

Now that she was my guest, I peppered her with stories of my exile. I watched her eyes as I detailed my life in the Hunan farm and the Shandong fishing boat. She was fascinated. Sometimes I caught her staring deeply at me, as if she wanted more. I gave her anecdote after anecdote, even as I scooped more dry-fried green beans on her bowl of rice. I watched with delight when she finally closed her eyes in surrender to the fiery taste of silky *mapo tofu*.

In the days that followed, I learned she had a boyfriend

in Manila, a graduate student who had recently moved to Washington, D.C. After visiting Beijing, she was all set to fly to the U.S., with a stop in D.C. I was undeterred. On the third week of her stay, I asked her to marry me.

"No," she said.

Beijing, she explained, was a mere stop on her way to the U.S. to spend the rest of the summer with her boyfriend.

I was crestfallen. And I thought that was that. I maintained contact but soon gave up on winning her heart. I heard stories about the kinds of dates she liked back in Manila: the suitors showing up in expensive cars and taking her to fancy restaurants. I thought of the other dates we had in Beijing: biking to cheap noodle houses. I guess that didn't work. I concluded that we were simply not meant for each other.

But at the end of that summer, she called me and said she was back in Beijing. She had abandoned her plans for law school, and instead secured a part-time job as a library and classroom teacher's aide at the International School of Beijing. She did not tell me immediately, but I soon learned that she had split from her boyfriend.

It was not a sharp turn toward romance, however. She went on sightseeing and food adventures with other people. She was not interested in committing to exclusive relationships — or at least not with me, I thought. She called whenever she wanted company or wanted an admirer's attention. I could supply that. She told me about several dates with other young men in Beijing. They weren't serious. But I saw myself turning into a best friend and confidante.

I went back to the Friday evening parties at the many embassies where I could meet potential dates. I got together with my wider circle of friends — Chinese acquaintances, former college schoolmates who found jobs in the business sector and new friends in the small coterie of journalists. I went out with women in these circles and started a relationship with an American lawyer. But I kept thinking of Ana. I kept imagining the future with her.

By springtime the following year, we had spent so much time together — traveling to Shanghai, Hangzhou and Suzhou with her sister Raissa — that I thought I had to try again. She knew all my friends. We'd grown accustomed to each other's quirks and temperament. We'd danced a lot.

We were sitting in an old, paisley hand-me-down sofa in my tiny sublet studio in *Qijiayuan*. I spoke in Filipino. "*Magpakasal na tayo*" I said. Let's get married. I offered no diamond ring. There was no getting down on one knee. There were no hidden friends jumping out with cameras to record the event.

"*Sige*," she said with a nod. Yes.

Later she'd compare my proposal to someone asking to borrow 20 *kuai* (roughly US$3). I said I thought her response was like agreeing to pay a street vendor the first asking price at Beijing's old Silk Alley. What, no bargaining?

Well, maybe a little bargaining. Several days after my proposal, I asked Ana to join me in a meeting with the Chinese housing authorities. I needed her, I said, to be part of my long-standing application for a new and bigger apartment. My conversation with the housing chief was full of formalities and bureaucratese and Ana could not follow the discussion. Minutes later, however, I was vigorously shaking hands with the housing chief, repeating "*haohaohao*" (good-good-good) and "*xiexie, xiexie*" (thank-you, thank-you) to each other.

When we stepped out of the office, I told Ana that the housing cadres had finally promised to get back to me soon about a new place. She asked what changed their attitude. I whispered, "I told them my girlfriend refused to marry me unless I had an apartment."

Weeks later, we were inspecting a two-bedroom rental: our first home.

In February 1986, Ferdinand Marcos was overthrown by a People Power revolution led by members of the military, the Catholic Church, and a populist uprising that crystalized around Corazon Aquino, the widow of the president's assassinated rival. With Marcos gone, my concerns about arrest and incarceration as a "leftist activist" were gone. But I returned to China because that was where my career—and much of my life—now was.

The Philippines saw the first of what turned out to be a series of popular revolts around the world that would culminate in the fall of the Berlin Wall and the fall of the Soviet Union. That wave would sweep into China itself beginning in April 1989 with the takeover of Tiananmen Square in Beijing by student activists. I covered the unprecedented public protests with Sandra Burton, who assumed the job of TIME's bureau chief after helping chronicle the fall of Marcos in the Philippines. She and I saw the parallels between China and the Philippines.

As I said, Xiao Jiang, the roommate who became one of my best friends, moved to Canada to teach. But what happened to the two others and some of my other classmates?

After completing his one-year special course in summer of 1979, my first roommate Zhang Jinwei, the Worker-Peasant-Soldier enrollee, went back to his old work unit, the Museum of Chinese History, taking up the same post and earning the same salary and socialist benefits.

"To me, life in Beida was something novel and fresh," he said, reminiscing thirty-five years after leaving the school. "I joined the army after high school, demobilized and got a job in the museum, and then got back into school. All our classmates were Communist Party members, all were achievers in their respective work units. We all cherished the chance to study in Beida, which was hard to come by."

After toiling for twenty-six years in the museum, Jinwei took early retirement in 2000. But he hasn't slowed down. He has organized exhibitions by China's top artists and calligraphers. He still holds three titles, including Secretary General of the China Association for Promotion of Exchanges with Chinese Painters and Calligraphers. He is the editor of an influential calligraphy and painting magazine published in Beijing and moderates important seminars in China's provinces, as well as in Hong Kong and Taiwan. "My workload now is still very big," he wrote to me on WeChat, China's main social messaging platform. That sentence was followed by eighteen emojis indicating great joy.

My third roommate, Li Xiaocong, or Lao Li, stuck to an academic career. After graduating in 1982, he stayed in Beida as a college instructor and secured a master's degree in history there in 1988, becoming, as he says, "a Beida lifer." He said, "I did not think of changing careers." Some specializations he attempted to pursue required advanced math, which he did not have and so failed to qualify for. But one demanding professor found much to value in Lao Li's experience during the Cultural Revolution: field surveying and map drawing skills from his time in Tibet.

"He asked me what kind of minerals we prospected in Tibet, and which period these deposits were from. He was impressed with my answers, so he agreed that I take an exam on history. I got in as his graduate student."

Soon, Lao Li was involved in the compilation of city maps that were forming into the massive and magisterial "Compendium of China's National Historical Maps." His work took twenty-eight years. The compendium was published to great academic acclaim in 2014. In the meantime, he had become a full professor with tenure.

But he still blames the Cultural Revolution for lost opportunities.

"My academic life turned out too short. I retired after only thirty years," he said. "My biggest regret is, I got into college a bit too late. The chaos of the Cultural Revolution stole ten years from my generation, depriving us of more opportunities to learn. We were not able to read enough books, our knowledge was not broad, and we could not keep up with our mentors."

He is philosophical, nevertheless.

"I caught the good period when China was just reversing course, correcting things, liberating the mind, and starting reform and open door. The ruling party had started to focus on economic construction, discarding 'class struggle.' We started to have enough food to eat. More meat on the dinner table. These were essentials that we did not dare dream of getting during the ten years of the Cultural Revolution."

Was it different for the women graduates? Perhaps something can be gleaned from the post-Beida life of my good friend Chen Yanni. She always looks younger than her age, which she does to this day. It belies the complexity of her experiences after leaving Beida. She got assigned her first job as a staff associate at the General Office of the Communist Party, the nerve-center of the ruling party, working in the section that dealt with people's complaints and grievances. Given that just about everything revolves around and is controlled by the Party, this was a plum entry-level job in terms of prestige and importance, if not perks. But that did not satisfy her. She moved to a state-run enterprise but was unhappy there too. In 1989, like an increasing number of classmates, she decided to move to the U.S. The takeover of Tiananmen Square by pro-democracy student groups helped her make up her mind.

"I made the decision to leave on May 13, 1989," she recalls.

"That afternoon I was in Tiananmen Square and watched those hunger striking students marching into the Square. I realized then that this is not the place in which I want to spend the rest of my life."

But, after moving to America, she remained unhappy. "I went through a harsh period, just like most Chinese students at that time. We didn't have money. We had to work to cover my living expenses. Years later, my husband remarked, 'A person who at age thirty-three went to a foreign country with a thousand dollars in the pocket and knew there was no fall back—I don't know if you were brave or stupid.' What kept me going? Beida spirit? I am not sure. I guess I didn't have any choice but move forward. One thing for sure is if I didn't go to Beida I would not be the person who I am now. Beida changed me completely."

She moved back and forth between the U.S. and China before finally returning in 2004. For the past years since she came back, she had tried to do business projects with friends. In 2008, she and a few partners tried to bring advanced American technology to China to treat city garbage. "The process was very hard and slower than what I like," she said, but their first project, a $650-million technology transfer was on the way to being built. She has also survived a bout with breast cancer. Waiting for that project to take off, she worked part-time as a bookkeeper at CNN's Beijing bureau.

Many Class '77 cohorts turned out to be high achievers, but there were three of my Beida schoolmates who aimed highest—looking not just to bring themselves to the most prominent of positions but to be able to change China itself. And that was part of the reason I would be in New York in 2014 looking for a man in the cage in Times Square.

12

RISING, WAYWARD, AND FALLEN STARS

IN 2014, when I found the cage in Times Square in the middle of New York City, there was no one in it. The day was gray but not cold; the district, which has become a messy pedestrian mall, was full of tourists, and people were hanging out on the stools and high tables that the city had set up in a desultory manner.

One person said the man in the cell had gone to get lunch, and I perused the pamphlets and notices tacked onto the cage: diatribes against the government, petitions in support of a dissident held by Beijing signed prominently by the co-chairman of the China Democratic Party, Wang Juntao, the man I had come to see. A star at Beida, he had followed a decidedly wayward trajectory upon graduation compared to other promising alumni, achieving notoriety and controversy, not fame and power in his homeland.

When Wang finally emerged from a side street, I noticed that he'd grown paunchier and balder since I last saw him in school. He had been one of the smartest kids in Beida, breezing through the *gaokao* without having to cram and fret like the other enrollees, and immediately being ushered into the most advanced classes in the university. He was just nineteen when he started college and he studied nuclear physics. I introduced myself as a Beida alumnus and we made small talk to figure out where each of us stood in terms of the Class of '77 (he was in the second batch that technically enrolled in 1978).

I told him I remembered his run for the Beijing district council seat back in 1980, in the abortive election that the government eventually nullified. He reminded me that as much as he was a science nerd, his first passion was politics. Even before enrolling in Beida, he'd been elected into the leadership of the Communist Youth League, a training ground for future communist leaders.

"I was lined up as a third-echelon future leader of the Communist Party, even ahead of Li Keqiang," he told me, referring to his Beida contemporary who is now the Chinese premier.

Even though he had been anointed an insider, Wang was a renegade. "I was imprisoned in 1976, at age seventeen, and jailed for 224 days for taking part in the April 5 Movement," he said, referring to the Tiananmen Square demonstration that spiraled out of mourning for Zhou Enlai. After Wang was released, he worked in the countryside for over a year. Then he took and passed the *gaokao* to become an *enfant terrible* in Beida.

The years hadn't mellowed him. Talking at full throttle in Times Square, Wang recalled how he morphed from a "*tizhi nei*" (political system insider) I to a "*tizhi wai*" (outsider) dissident. "In 1979, when the authorities started persecuting dissidents, I gave up on them," he said, referring to the crackdown on the Democracy Wall movement. "For me the most important lesson from the Cultural Revolution was to stop political persecution. If you did that again, I would not go along with you."

After graduating from Beida, in 1985, he co-founded the Beijing Social and Economic Research Institute, China's first independent think-tank. It was active in advising the students who led the takeover of Tiananmen Square in early 1989. We were probably in the Square at the same time—I, reporting for TIME magazine; he, counseling and strategizing with the students trying to change China.

In the immediate aftermath of the crackdown, Wang fled south to the city of Wuhan and then attempted to reach Guangdong Province, from which he could presumably try to get to Hong Kong. But the authorities caught up with him and, after a quick trial in 1990, he was given a thirteen-year sentence, convicted as one of the "black hands" who had organized the Tiananmen protests. After four years—and as Washington was about to decide whether to renew China's most-favored nation trade status—he was released on medical parole and promptly bundled off to the United States. In exile, he earned post-graduate degrees in political science at Harvard and Columbia University.

"Armed uprisings aside, I've done all kinds of anti-establishment projects in a communist state," he said as he prepared to get back into his cage in Times Square. "And I did very well. Now I am looking forward to resuming those."

Daily life for him involves a bit of commute. He lives in Holmdel, a New Jersey town one hour's drive from Manhattan but that doesn't seem to faze him. Brushing forward his thinning black hair with a hand, he launched into a boilerplate political attack on Beijing, with the kind of stentorian style that Beijing officials often use against their own political targets. Sitting on the cardboard floor of the makeshift cage, he explained his mission to anyone who asked, passing out leaflets with more information.

There has been no letup in Wang's uber-activism. He still serves as chairman of the National Committee of Democratic Party of China. In summer of 2021, he texted me: "Every Saturday, we demonstrate for China's democracy at Times Square. We protest against Chinese Communist tyranny, demonstrating in front of China's consulate in NYC and the embassy in Washington

DC." Wang remains feisty. "In the past years, China and the world have undergone dramatic changes. I can see a great storm coming soon." He tried to sum up what Beida alumni were about: "We care more about thinking or ideology than political achievements."

That may be how Wang was looking at what his ambitions and his achievements have come to. But it is not true for some of our other classmates. Many of the graduates of Peking University—aware that they have a reputation to uphold, of being in the vanguard of everything—have plenty of political achievement. Beida's political exemplar in this era is Li Keqiang. He is currently the second most powerful politician in China, ranking number two in the Communist Party's leadership and, as Premier, the de facto CEO of the second biggest economy in the world.

I never knew Li in school but other friends of mine at school did. And I would later meet him as I covered Chinese politics. The school connection helped to warm up the conversation, but he has always tended to speak cautiously in public. He has the kind of polite gregariousness you expect from politicians, engaging and friendly but ultimately controlled. He doesn't have the tightly-wound, ready-to-debate personality of Wang Juntao. Indeed, he seems to calibrate his demeanor to circumstances: when he makes official appearances at the Great Hall of the People with President Xi Jinping—China's most powerful politician—the taller Li is expressionless, almost dour, and slightly hunched. But in more relaxed arenas, he can be spontaneous. During small talk after a panel at the World Economic Forum in Davos in 2015, he engaged in a colloquial and fluent, if slightly halting, conversation in English with other attendees.

For Li, English was a serious pursuit at school. "Keqiang was tireless in studying English, to the point that young people nowadays would find hard to imagine," He Qinhua, one of his classmates wrote in a memoir. "He recited it while walking, while queued up at the canteen, while on the bus and waiting for the bus." A student in the law department, he would translate into Chinese *The Due Process of Law*, a seminal book on legal theory by the British jurist Alfred Denning. The translation, on which he collaborated with Yang Baikui, an international relations major at Beida, was published and was recently reissued.

"He was quite open-minded and inclusive," recalled Yang Baikui. "He was even friends with Wang Juntao. It's a mark of his political skills." However, Yang said Li was so single-minded he did not even go out drinking with schoolmates after class. "He wanted to be a politician and in China politicians have no friends." Wang, the firebrand, remembers he saw something potentially revolutionary in the future politician. "The Li Keqiang I knew was bold and idealistic," Wang said when we talked in New York. But Li took another political road, and while Wang was seated in a self-made cage to make a point in New York City, Li was seated in the chair of the Premier of China.

Born in July 1955, Li was the son of a minor official in Anhui, a poor rural province in eastern China. After finishing high school in 1974, he worked for four years on a farm near his hometown until the *gaokao* was restored. Passing was one thing, deciding which university to apply to was another. In his memoir, Li recalled his dilemma when he had to fill in his "three wishes" — his school preferences — in the *gaokao* application form. A few days earlier, a friend who was a Beida alumnus advised him to "cherish this once-in-ten-years opportunity and make Beida your one and only choice."

But Li hesitated and instead put down his hometown's teachers college as his first choice. "If I went there, I was told, I won't need to spend for meals," he wrote in "The Story of Beida and I," an essay published by the *China Youth Daily* in 2015. "Still, I had an irresistible yearning towards Beida so I wrote down Beida as my second choice." Li scored high and so, despite being his second choice, Beida accepted him.

Li was cautious even as he strategized what life would be like after graduation. In their senior year, Li and his classmates had the chance to take special exams for graduate studies abroad.

"I remember discussing the pros and cons with KQ and other classmates," recalled Liu Fengming, who referred to his classmate with the initials of his given name. "We all thought that if KQ chose to take the exams, he would pass with flying colors."

But Li chose to remain in China, and in Beida, where step by step he climbed the ladder of the Communist Youth League, an important training ground for communist officials. He rose as a national official of the CYL while completing a master's degree in law at Beida and then finished an economics doctorate under the tutelage of Li Yining, a Beida professor who advocated market reforms.

Eventually, Li became the protégé of top communist leaders like Hu Jintao, who later rose to become Communist Party chief and China's leader. In power for ten years, Hu placed Li on a fast track to political stardom, with the potential of rising to the top leadership post itself. In 1998, Li, only 33, became one of the youngest provincial governors in China, when he was sent to oversee Henan Province, one of the biggest and poorest in the country. In 2004, he was made party chief of Liaoning, a rust-belt province seeking investment and growth. Just as Li began his tenure in that province, a schoolmate Bo Xilai was leaving office as party chief of Dalian, one of Liaoning's biggest cities, to become Minister of Commerce in Beijing. The careers of Bo and Li would intersect in many ways: while both had Beida in their intellectual lineage, they had allied themselves to different factions in China's power structure. Li was a protégé of Hu Jintao; Bo owed allegiance to Jiang Zemin, Hu's predecessor as paramount leader of China.

In November 2013, at age 58, Li was promoted to the No. 3 position in the Communist Party. But he would not become No. 1, as that would go to someone else. In 2013, in accordance with the secret and carefully-crafted succession plans negotiated by the various factions of the regime, he was promoted to be China's premier. Bo's career, in the meantime, was to provide drama, scandal, and political fireworks.

I was working for TIME magazine when I caught up with Bo in 1998. I hadn't seen him since school and, when we met up, he had been mayor of Dalian, a port city on the peninsular tip of Liaoning province, for five years. Under his administration, the city had won a reputation for being not only economically sound—chalking up double-digit annual growth—but also green. The magazine was doing a story on China's looming environmental crisis and Dalian would fit perfectly into the coverage as a city that was doing things right.

I didn't mention the Beida connection when I applied to the Dalian foreign affairs office for permission to report on the city. I asked to visit a few places, talk with local experts and interview Mayor Bo. I also provided the kind of questions I intended to ask. These were all standard practice for conducting any kind of journalistic coverage in China.

The Dalian foreign affairs functionaries replied a day or two later. I was told the mayor would be happy to meet me. I showed up in the city government building in central Dalian and was ushered into a large meeting hall. Several heavily cushioned chairs were arranged in a U-shape. On one side sat four men all dressed in business suits. They introduced themselves as local officials from various departments. It seemed to be the traditional set-up for the stiff, uncomfortable, totally unrevealing Chinese government interview.

I was politely chatting with the functionaries when Bo walked in, followed by a young woman, who was his translator. We shook hands and he hugged me. *"Hao jiu bu jian!"* (Long time no see!), Bo exclaimed. He turned to the four officials, who were standing at attention, and told them how we had known each other some fifteen years earlier as Class of '77 classmates in Beida's history department. They nodded and said "Ah." Bo then told the four that they could leave now. A little startled at being dismissed, they meekly and awkwardly departed, leaving only the translator, who sat behind the table that separated my seat from Bo's. For the first ten minutes or so, Bo and I chatted in Chinese, talking about our time in Beida and, one by one, updating each other about our mutual friends in the class. How is so and so? What has she been up to lately? Where does he work now? Is he married yet?

Then the official interview began, with the translator quietly taking notes and my cassette recorder rolling. It turned out to be remarkably candid and relaxed — surprising for an official, particularly the mayor of a huge city. For one thing, he admitted that back in 1993, when he became mayor, he was not particularly sensitive to environmental issues.

"I merely had a deep affection for Dalian and wished to turn it into a nice-looking artistic creation," he said. But in pursuit of that goal, he slowly evolved into a defender of the environment: planting trees, shutting down polluting factories, dredging the river.

He described phoning local officials directly to clean things up. "I will do so even if they are asleep. People will carry out orders immediately if it comes from the mayor." He said he liked to tear down walls — literally. "Chinese gardens are good," he told me, "but you can only see them once inside the walls. By tearing down the walls, residents can see greenery every day."

Born a couple of months before Mao proclaimed the foundation of the People's Republic, Bo had an illustrious Communist Party lineage. His father Bo Yibo was one of the more senior military figures in Mao's Red Army. Bo Yibo was also a major player in the Byzantine politics of Beijing post-takeover — and as such became a target for the radical leftists who spearheaded the Cultural Revolution. Bo Yibo was publicly humiliated, divested of his official titles and imprisoned for a dozen years, during which time he was tortured. It was a horrific experience for his son as well. Bo Yibo's wife, Xilai's mother, was beaten to death by the Red Guards. Bo Xilai, one story went, may have been forced to publicly denounce his father. That did not prevent the younger man from being thrown into prison as well.

When I first met him at Beida, everyone knew of Bo's upbringing and the purging of his father during the Cultural Revolution. Everyone expected Bo Yibo to be rehabilitated by Deng Xiaoping's reformist regime. But when school started, it was not yet official. And so the "princeling" — a term used for the children of the party elders — began his Beida studies under a cloud.

At Beida, Bo and I took classes together, even though he majored in world history while I studied Chinese history. Tall and good-looking, he stood out in class, even if he usually came in class wearing the ubiquitous Mao jacket and baggy pants. We sometimes would lunch together at the No. 36 cafeteria, chowing down the usual fare of sauteed cabbage with strips of fatty pork, pickled radish and steamed *mantou* (wheat buns). Bo always struck up conversations with the foreign students because he liked to talk about international affairs and to improve his

English.

He treated his Chinese schoolmates differently. Class '77 alumnus Bai Weiji said, "He was polite and nice to his classmates but he also kept us at arms' length. Maybe this was because his father had not been fully rehabilitated at the time. Bo had natural charisma, which he showed more and more after his father returned to power late in 1978."

In spite of his lineage, Bo's career goal as a Beida student was fairly modest: he wanted to become a foreign correspondent for China's state media. And so, after just over a year in Beida, he took another entrance exam and transferred to the Chinese Academy of Social Sciences in a newly-launched master's program in journalism. There was no farewell party. Bo just completed his Beida program and quietly moved out of campus.

But Bo was destined for politics. His father was rehabilitated with full honors and was also praised as being one of the country's "Eight Immortals" — the wise men of the Communist Party who counseled Deng on the reforms that were transforming China. The elder Bo actively promoted his son through the system. After working briefly in the Communist Party's Central Committee Office in Beijing, Bo Xilai was appointed county magistrate in northeastern China. Shortly after, he became mayor of Dalian, where we would have our reunion.

Bo's success with Dalian led to his appointment as governor of the entire Liaoning province in 2001. Year 2002 brought an even more momentous promotion: entry to the central committee, the senior body of the Communist Party. He moved back to Beijing to become the minister of trade and commerce. The week he was promoted, a dozen of us, history classmates of Beida's Class of '77, gathered in a Beijing restaurant for a rare reunion. Bo was among us. We found him less exuberant than before, reticent and cautious, especially when we asked about his prospects. He had become more of a government official, guarding his words. But he still exuded charisma. He did not hesitate to make small talk, shaking hands and patting shoulders, keenly asking what we were doing in our personal lives.

"He was a fusion of a Western politician and a Chinese princeling with the qualities of an international affairs reporter," said Bai Weiji, who was also at the lunch.

We would all watch from afar as our classmate rose even higher. In 2007, Bo was given a seat on the 25-person Politburo of the Communist Party—which ran the country— and also appointed party chief of Chongqing, a booming megacity in central China. There he made a splash by promoting two startling campaigns—one a high-profile crackdown on crime and local triads, the other an effort to revive nostalgia for the Chinese communist past, including the public singing of "red songs" in praise of Mao Zedong. That disturbed many Chinese, including Beida classmates, who remembered the torturous years of the Cultural Revolution all too painfully. Still, some of us gave him the benefit of the political doubt: we argued that Bo was resorting to these campaigns as a tactic to enhance his political standing in the leadership.

"I didn't think that he was a real Maoist deep down," Bai Weiji said. "He was merely doing it to win popular support and gain political points."

Indeed, Bo seemed to be aiming for the highest of offices—the head of the Communist Party itself. But in February 2012, the police chief of Chongqing, one of Bo's most trusted lieutenants, suddenly showed up at the U.S. consulate in Chengdu to ask for political asylum and offering to inform on his boss. A messy scandal then revealed itself. Bo's wife Gu Kailai, herself a princeling and a Class of '79 law graduate from Beida, was arrested for the murder of a British businessman named Neil

Heywood. She was tried in 2014 and given a suspended death sentence. In September that same year, Bo was tried and sentenced to life in prison for alleged corruption and abuse of power. Chinese state media — which Bo Xilai had once aspired to work for — and the foreign press delved into his family life, exposing the lavish lifestyle of the family including the allegedly playboy ways of their son Bo Guagua, then studying for a master's degree at Harvard University.

Several weeks before his parents were tried in China, I met up with Guagua in Los Angeles, where he was on a brief visit. He agreed to meet me, knowing that I was a former Beida classmate of his father. He came alone when we met over coffee in the food court section of the Westfield Topanga Mall. "So did you drive over in a red Ferrari or Porsche," I joked. "No," he replied, grinning. "I drove a Mazda that I borrowed from an L.A. friend."

I expected to meet a flashy, boisterous brat. He disappointed. He was casually dressed and good looking, but he was neither brash nor loud. Speaking in fluent English, he talked to me "off the record", sharing background information, his thoughts and his family's side of the case. He denied allegations of corruption and profligate living made against his family as "media gossip". He described the case against them as "politically motivated". I tried to convince him to write their side of the story so I could get it published in CNN's website or other platforms. He agreed to think about it but days later he declined. "I care most about my parents' well-being, especially my mother's," he said. "I do not think publishing one now would help."

Soon after earning his law degree from Columbia Law School in 2016, Guagua passed the New York state bar. In 2019, he moved to Canada to work for Power Corporation, a company owned by the Desmarais family, who have remained friends with the Bo family for many years. Bo and his wife today languish in jail, Bo in Qincheng, a prison near Beijing long used for the incarceration of high-profile political prisoners, and his wife in a women's prison in Beijing.

The irony is that while both Li and Bo aimed for the number one spot in China, the winner of the contest would be Xi Jinping, a "Worker-Peasant-Soldier" student from Tsinghua University, Beida's great rival just a block away in Beijing. In fact, despite Beida's pride of place in history and culture, it is the graduates of Tsinghua — mostly trained engineers — who have been most successful in politics in recent decades, coopting ideas that may have been first conceived around Weiming Hu, the Lake with No Name. It is also ironic that Xi, as the leader of China, would reinstitute the nostalgia for the Maoist past, which Bo Xilai had tried to do to great controversy in his own heyday.

13

GAOKAO TODAY

BACK IN 1977, the re-institution of the *gaokao* was a godsend. Suddenly, the opportunity for education and advancement in the country's best universities was available to millions of politically disenfranchised citizens — the children of class enemies in the Cultural Revolution, those without the political connections that could guarantee them places in those schools, the offspring of the purged. That is what made the Class of '77 such a pioneering generation: the revival of hope for the future.

Today, college entrance is different. Even though high school students devote at least a year prepping for the test, *gaokao* no longer has the desperate quality it possessed back at the end of the Cultural Revolution. It is still important, but no longer an extraordinary event; and the educational system actively directs students toward taking it.

Long gone are the days when young people would be sent down to the countryside as a primary part of their education, but most students take some form of after-school classes in order to get extra practice to help them pass exams. It is now easier to get into a Chinese university because they have vastly expanded their enrollment numbers. And besides the colleges and universities, China has over the years opened technical and vocational schools offering specialized training in employable trades like culinary courses, bartending and dressmaking.

There has been much talk of reforming the *gaokao*, and cutting the memorization aspect that takes up most of the energy of the year of prep work high school students go through. Educators also want to make the *gaokao* more equitable. The practice of giving local residents first dibs on local colleges means that young people in, say, Beijing get to be first in line to the best schools in the country, including Beida and Tsinghua. The young people I spoke to thought using different standards for students from different provinces was indeed unfair, as well as giving bonus points to ethnic minorities. But otherwise, they thought it was mostly fair. They agreed too that pieces of paper couldn't really test what a person is really made of.

But there is another phenomenon taking place. Some of the best students are skipping *gaokao* entirely because it does nothing to help them get into the universities they want to attend, which aren't in China. Others are being encouraged not to go to college at all, but rather to go to vocational schools—China's higher education is now producing more graduates than the economy can use. But the global focus of many young Chinese, and indeed their parents, will remain in place. The wave of Chinese students going overseas may ebb and flow but they are likely to continue to be an important source of income for universities in English-speaking countries in the West.

Those of the generation after the chaos of the Cultural Revolution who earned a college education still feel a great sense of gratitude. Huang Nubo is a case in point. I hadn't seen him for thirty years. He had been one of the "country bumpkins," from the Beida class that preceded the revival of the *gaokao*. And as much as alumni from the Class of '77 onward may look askance at the Worker-Peasant-Soldier Beida graduates, Huang is as proud of his academic pedigree as they are.

But he has been far more successful than most of them. In fact, he has been so successful that Beida and the people there have become the beneficiaries of the largesse he has accumulated as the founder and chairman of Beijing Zhongkun Investment Group, a real estate and resort company.

We were reunited in a Chinese New Year get-together among alumni and his company's executives. As is the Chinese style, we proceeded to have a banquet. Over an eight-course meal, we caught up with each other. We'd both roomed in Building 26, where I was paired up with Zhang Jinwei while he was assigned to room with a soft-spoken but gregarious student from Iceland. Huang was tall, lanky, and athletic. I often saw him in jogging suits going or coming from an early morning run. He was a member of the varsity track team, a 110-meter hurdle specialist.

He was now much less athletic and had put on weight. He didn't look like the hurdler he once was. Still, Huang told me, he works out daily, running and doing weights in the gym. Over our dinner, he gave me three autographed copies of his books that he'd chosen out of the dozen volumes he had published under the name Luo Wen. They were written as poems. "One is about my childhood, growing up in Ningxia," he explained, referring to one of the poorest provinces in China. "Another is a diary of my experiences during the Cultural Revolution, and the third is a book of poems on my mountaineering expeditions." He has climbed Kilimanjaro once and Everest three times. He has also been to the North Pole.

Huang was born in 1956 in Gansu Province, a remote and desolate region in northwest China, and grew up in neighboring Ningxia. During the Cultural Revolution, his father, a soldier, was vilified as a "counter-revolutionary" and was banished to a local Gulag, where he died of starvation. His mother died suddenly when he was thirteen. During those tumultuous years,

Huang said, he lived like a vagabond, begging in the streets.

Huang changed his fate by first changing his given name. One day, when he was sixteen, while standing beside the Yellow River, he watched the waves smash against the riverbanks. That day, he decided to change his given name—Yuping (Jade Peace) to Nubo (Angry Wave). He was livid at the unfortunate turns in his life but was going to use his fury to energize his future. He joined volunteer youth crews working on farms and was accepted as a member of the Communist Party at age eighteen. As one of the anointed, he was admitted into Beida in 1976 as a Worker-Peasant-Soldier student. From 1976-81, he studied in the Chinese department, where he learned literature and creative writing and received a bachelor's degree.

After graduation, Huang got a sinecure in the Ministry of Propaganda, an influential agency which meant financial security for life. He rose to become a section chief, but after ten years working in the bureaucracy, he decided to "*xiahai*"—jump into the sea of private entrepreneurship.

"I came out like a blind man," he told me. "I was very naïve." He sold toys, printed name cards and later peddled copying machines. He got cheated making his first big transaction trading a consignment of iron and steel and had to fight back, with bluster and threats, to recover his capital. In 1996, he decided to get serious about learning the art of deal-making. He took a two-year Executive Master's program in business administration from the China-Europe International Business School (CEIBS).

"Coming out of the bureaucracy, I was freer," he told me. "I had no constraints, no pressure." Bagging one real estate deal after another, Huang has emerged as one of China's richest entrepreneurs. His company owns property and resorts in China and overseas, including some in Los Angeles and Nashville.

But Huang had his share of miscues. He kept in touch with

his Icelandic roommate, Hjörleifur Sveinbjörnsson, who had married a woman who would become Mayor of Reykjavik. Ever a risk-taking entrepreneur, Huang had pursued deals in that faraway country. In 2011, he caused a furor when he tried to buy a sparsely populated but scenic piece of land—300 square kilometers (190 square miles)—hoping to invest $200 million to develop a resort with a hotel, golf course and horse-riding facilities. He had envisioned it as a base to attract affluent Chinese tourists, but Icelandic officials foiled his bid, citing national security concerns. Huang's plan fell victim to a deep suspicion, or paranoia, about China's growing global influence. "It was purely business," Huang said.

He is a serious philanthropist and has donated funds for the preservation of Xidi and Hongcun, ancient villages and UNESCO World Heritage sites in Anhui Province. He has set up scholarships for Beida students and a professorial chair at the China Europe International Business School (CEIBS) in Shanghai. He also paid for a new courtyard-style building on Beida campus which now houses the World Poetry Academy, which he helped set up. His favorite Chinese literature professor at Beida runs the academy as president. Huang has pledged to leave a big chunk of his wealth to his employees and to Beida. He told me he expects to give Beida at least one billion yuan, or about US$158 million, in donations. "You must give back to the society," he said. "Beida changed my life, from a child beggar to a world-hopping entrepreneur, adventurer and poet. Beida's education inspired me."

POSTSCRIPT

AFTER five decades of living and working in the People's Republic, I realize I've become part of the fabric of China—even though I am at my core still Filipino. The years have woven me into the life of the country where I once thought I was a castaway, exiled and longing to return home to my family. Now I can come and go as I please, but remarkably, China has become my second home.

Many Chinese also associate me with their country. On a flight between Beijing and Ningxia—the arid region in China's northwest—I was a little unnerved by a fellow passenger on the plane who kept staring at me. Finally, a little shyly, he introduced himself. He said he was a fan. "I remember you," he said. "And I'm very grateful."

He was referring to my work in the early 1980s as part of the *English on Sunday* TV show. That passenger seated near me on the plane, Han Zhaofang, had recognized me three decades after the show was on the air. At the time the program was broadcast, he was a college student. "I learned and improved my English watching you on English on Sunday on Chinese TV," Han told me. "That was in the 1980s. I especially remember you, typically playing the guitar and singing with your group." By this time, Han, 60, had become the manager of a government agency in Beijing promoting paragliding as a sport.

I gave up being a full-time journalist in 2015 when I retired as Beijing bureau chief for CNN. But I haven't left China. I still keep a residence in Beijing and spend half of my time there. More poignantly, however, I have returned to Beida.

After leaving CNN, I gave talks about China's economic and social evolution to groups in the mainland, the Philippines and others in the region—the Young Presidents Organization's annual meeting in Hangzhou, the Rotary Club in Manila, the East-West Center in Hawaii, and the American Apparel & Footwear Association's meeting in Hong Kong. Professors at Beida took notice and, in 2017, the school invited me to become an adjunct professor at the School of Journalism and Communications. I teach "China and Media Matters" for one semester a year.

The syllabus covers the country's metamorphosis from socialist dystopia to rising global power, as well as the role and responsibilities of journalism in China, the power of images, the ever-changing media landscape in the country and the world, the promise and pitfalls of new media, and the importance of critical thinking and ethics. It's China 101 plus journalism, an intersection of Chinese contemporary history with China reporting. It's an elective course, which means students choose to take it because they are keenly interested in the topics, not just to earn required academic credits. It's always a contentious and controversial set of issues. But my Chinese students—who make up about half the class with the rest from overseas—are among the smartest in the country and they know how to engage in debate. After all, that's why they wanted to get into Beida in the first place.

Physically, Beida is pretty much the school I first visited in August 1971 when the Great Proletarian Cultural Revolution was still underway. The campus is just as much a refuge from the big city as then—charming with its lush gardens, quaint courtyards and serene pathways, which resemble the traditional architecture and gardens of the nearby Old Summer Palace. Several structures from the end of the 19th century—pavilions, gazebos, stone bridges—have been preserved. The iconic structure remains the pagoda-style Boya Tower—which was built in 1924 as an elaborate water reservoir but is now completely decorative. It still stands next to the *Weiming Hu* (literally, Lake Without A Name), around which the school has planted weeping willows, shrubs, flowering trees, and set up more wooden benches, making the famous lake appear cleaner and greener than it was when I was a student. Flocks of mandarin ducks and schools of red koi populate the lake. However, it is also less tranquil. Quite often, especially during national holidays, hordes of visitors flock here for rounds of selfies. Parents drag their small children along its banks as if they were on a campus tour, to impress on them the importance of attending the premier institution of higher learning in the country. When winter freezes its surface, Weiming Lake becomes a favorite and crowded venue for skaters. And so, the tower and the lake have endured as the visual symbols of Beida since the school moved to this site, growing ever more popular in the Chinese imagination.

Some of the university's landmark edifices —though not necessarily the most appealing ones—have disappeared or been transformed. Gone is Building 26, the gray brick dormitory where I lived for three years in the 1970s. It was the residence for male foreign students until 2009, when it was torn down to make way for the five-story Beida Chinese Language Teaching School, which was opened in 2014 to house classrooms and lecture halls for overseas students learning Mandarin. No more dormitory buildings exclusively for male foreign students; most foreign students are assigned rooms outside the campus in multi-story hostel-like dormitories where they are assigned rooms. Others share rooms in houses rented privately from Chinese homeowners.

For Chinese students, accommodations at the residence halls have improved only marginally since my years at Beida. Back then, six Chinese students shared one small room and were crammed into bunk beds. Nowadays, four share a similar-sized room and each student is provided with a stand-alone bed and a desk.

"My dorm is quite small, and it has barely changed in the past sixty years," said Jia Ruimin, a second-year student at Beida's Medical School who took my China Media Matters course.

One major improvement: the bathrooms are now cleaned by professional janitors and, unlike my time, offer a choice of squat toilets — for Chinese students accustomed to such latrines — and Western-style porcelain thrones.

Building 26 had a twin: Building 25, which was reserved for female foreign students. It, too, is gone. In its place stands another five-story structure, painted beige and housing a complex of classrooms, lecture halls, a library and office space. It's the Mong Man Wai Building, named after a Hong Kong philanthropist. It houses the School of Journalism and Communications where I share an office on the third floor reserved for visiting scholars and professors.

Behind Building 26 used to be the Foreign Student's Cafeteria, a nondescript one-story structure. It's gone, too, replaced by the May 4th Sports Stadium, a four-story affair equipped with a swimming pool, badminton courts and indoor track. Eradicated as well is the big canteen — officially known as Cafeteria No. 36 — where I often lunched with Chinese classmates and where we often went ballroom dancing in the evening. Demolished in 1999, it is now the site of the Millennium Theater, a marble-and-stone auditorium reserved for large meetings, conferences, operas, ballets and cultural performances.

Next door is one of the most politically significant hubs in Beida history: *Sanjiaodi*, or The Triangle. Until 2017, *Sanjiaodi* had a bookstore, a post office, a convenience store, a barber shop and ample wall space where students posted announcements, advertisements, lost-and-found notes and, most significantly, the big-character posters that were often the way radicals announced major and often violent political campaigns against their enemies during the Cultural Revolution. Those walls are now gone, replaced by manicured grass, bushes and trees. Near the garden is the only vestige of the *Sanjiaodi* I used to know: an old, glass-covered bulletin board, some twenty meters long, displaying a list of outstanding students from various departments.

One thing that hasn't really changed is the rivalry between Beida and Tsinghua University. Every year, soon after the *gaokao* results are made public, both schools send teams of officials to seek out the national exam's top-notchers to entice them to their respective universities, dangling full scholarships, teaching assistantships, special living conditions and different types of other emoluments.

The rivalry is manifest in competing institutions in both schools. At Beida, the old No. 2 Sports Gymnasium, where my varsity basketball team used to practice in the late 1970s, has become a complex reconfigured for scholars of the Yenching Academy, which was inaugurated in 2015. Yenching — the name Beida had when it was first founded — was inspired both by the academies that thrived during China's centuries-old Confucian tradition and the Rhodes Scholarship at Oxford University. Every year, Yenching selects around 120 scholars — about 65% international students, the rest Chinese — for one or two years of study, at the end of which they get a master's degree. It is funded with Chinese government subsidies and private donations from Chinese entrepreneurs, including *Beida* alumni.

Yenching goes head-to-head against Schwarzman College at Tsinghua University, a similar Rhodes-like global scholarship founded and co-funded by Stephen Schwarzman, chairman and CEO of The Blackstone Group, the U.S.-based financial powerhouse. Schwarzman believes that future global leaders need to better understand China through immersive study in the country. At Tsinghua, scholars stay in a brand-new building and undertake a year of study, travel and cultural immersion, leading to a master's degree. Some 45% of the scholars are from the U.S., 20% from China, and 35% from the rest of the world. The program is funded by Schwarzman's initial $100 million donation made in 2013, and supplemented by a campaign that has since collected over $500 million.

Beida being Beida—that is, proud of its legacy of activism and debate—the Yenching program since its inception has been bedeviled by internal criticism from the university's students and faculty. They say offering Yenching's courses —which are in addition to existing classes at Beida—in English is a signal that the program is not inclusive enough of Chinese culture and language. Students also consider it unfair that Yenching scholars can get a master's degree in one year, instead of two, and worry that the Yenching degrees may diminish the prestige of Beida's. They bristled at what they saw as *tequan*, or "special rights," being granted to foreigners—an echo of the immunities and extraterritorial rights enjoyed by Westerners and the Japanese in the first half of the 20th century that made Chinese feel like second-class citizens in their own country, a humiliation that rankles to this day.

The Chinese students were irked by other things from the beginning of the Yenching program. Beida's plan had been to locate the Yenching campus-within-the-campus in Jing Yuan, a Qing dynasty-era garden encompassing six heritage buildings with bright red traditional entrances, trellises, and ornamental ivy on the walls. The Academy's architectural blueprint called for excavating the garden to install an underground complex of classrooms, lecture halls and dormitories, one that stretched downward multiple stories. Because of the proximity to the Old Summer Palace, the school is not allowed to build high-rises in the northern part of the campus. While that hampers Beida's expansion plans, it has spared it from the wrecking ball of China's often mindless drive to tear down and "modernize."

The school's plan was always to re-create the garden eventually, but students were outraged by the repurposing of the green spaces. Some thought the plan could spoil the beautiful old buildings. Their opposition compelled the university to abort its plan. And so the Academy took over Gym No. 2 instead. The blueprint for brand-new basement living spaces was scrapped. Yenching scholars instead stayed in spruced up dormitory rooms in one section of the Shaoyuan Hotel, a cheap but cheerful hostel built in 1981. It's adjacent to another, still-standing old dormitory where I lived during my senior year at Beida.

The pushback typified Beida's long tradition of political activism and non-conformity, one that dates back to the May 4th Movement, to the Cultural Revolution and to the Tiananmen protests of 1989. In comparison, the reaction at Tsinghua to the Schwarzman program was muted, consistent with the university's stereotypical image as a status quo conformist school for engineers and technocrats.

That's not to say Beida's student body hasn't changed as China has undergone its massive economic and cultural transformation. The country's prosperity — and the social media revolution that attends it — is etched into everything. Today, as in my time, bicycles are the norm, but they're different. I see students zipping by on ride-sharing bikes, electric motorbikes, and scooters, on their way to and from classes.

The millennial cohort exudes self-confidence, unlike the shell-shocked post-Cultural Revolution class of 1977. They dress in a wide range of clothing, from jeans, tees and hoodies to trendy outfits and fashion-forward frocks. They show no qualms about public displays of affection. That is a stark contrast with the students of my time, who on average were much older (mid to late-twenties, even early thirties) and wore monochromatic, unisex Mao jackets and loose pants. Back in the 1970s, students carried books, notebooks and chopsticks in PLA-style satchel bags. Now they lug their laptops and battery-chargers in Herschel-style backpacks.

My classmates and I had very little choice in terms of courses to take, books to read, places to live and things to do after the school day was over. Today, the range of choices expands constantly, online and off.

In the late 1970s and 1980s, we had poorly lit cafeterias offering rice porridge or millet gruel, or steamed buns paired with a dish of boiled cabbage sprinkled with strips of fatty pork and pickled radish. You might be able to cook your own food, but everything was in short supply. Cooking oil, grain and other staples were strictly rationed. Today, food choices are virtually limitless. There are half-a-dozen cafeterias on campus where, for as little as US$3, students can get *jiaozi* (dumplings) or Sichuanese twice-cooked pork or Cantonese-style noodles or other specialties from China's many regions, or Western fast food. And, of course, you can always order from online services, which promptly deliver from area restaurants to the school gates. If students prefer, they can also hang out in privately run cafes on and off campus like the Paradiso, which offers brewed coffee, soft drinks, sandwiches and snacks. There is free Wi-Fi everywhere.

My media classes are usually attended by over thirty students. About half are Chinese; the rest are exchange students from Canada, the United States, Britain, Italy, Austria, Singapore, Thailand and other places. More than 50% are female. Though the course is offered by the School of Journalism and Communication, fewer than a dozen of them plan to be journalists. Most are taking courses in the international politics, literature and history departments; many are enrolled in the Guanghua Business School or are training to be doctors. Many of them seek to know how the media in China and overseas work and how to use that knowledge in their chosen careers.

Some students were not even looking to satisfy academic credits. Jingjing Xiao asked to audit my class in January 2018 after hearing me give a talk on my career at the Bookworm, a wonderful library-bookstore-café that closed in 2019. Jingjing was a Yale exchange student at Beida's rival, Tsinghua University, who wanted to write about her grandfather. When he was a teenager, he joined and completed the Long March, the strategic retreat of the Red Army led by Mao Zedong that was key to their survival and eventual victory in 1949.

My course was oversubscribed—especially with Beida students who needed the credits—but she was relentless. "Your work was such an inspiration to my work!" she emailed me again and again. I agreed.

Every week, she rode her bicycle from her Tsinghua dormitory to sit in my weekly evening lectures. She missed only two sessions because she had to travel to Chengdu to do research on her grandfather's history.

The next year, in August 2021, Jingjing returned to Beijing after earning her Yale degree, this time to start a master's program at Beida. She also got into the prestigious Yenching Academy scholarship. She's already signed her first book deal.

I can't say I helped with that. "This is not a writing course," I always tell my new students. "I will not teach how to write well or how to master grammar. Other professors can help you with that." One of my few writing requirements is this: Every week, I ask them to put down brief essays – of no more than 200 words in clear, concise English – on the news or ongoing controversies. To be concise, I tell them, is to be an effective communicator.

Throughout the course, I offer them my long experience and perspective as an international journalist who has covered China for print and television. I teach the class what it takes to be a good reporter, what makes for good storytelling, how journalists do their jobs and why. I talk about the power of words and sound and images. I talk about the influence and perils of social media, the importance of ethics and the ills of censorship. I encourage debate.

I try to impart two pieces of advice to my students. One: Train yourself in critical thinking and writing; get past the smoke and mirrors, get to the hidden truth. Two: Aim high and work hard but be prepared for ups and downs. I survived the Cultural Revolution. You can get through your problems, too.

But can they? The generations have brought on a remarkable transformation.

In 2016, Ana bought two front-row tickets to a Bruno Mars concert in Beijing. I was aware of his Filipino ancestry, but I wasn't familiar with his music. The Chinese audience was. It was remarkable to hear the mostly young audience sing along.

It made me recall the young Chinese I had met over five decades – the Red Guards in Beijing in 1971, the re-educated youth in Hunan's state farm in 1972, my ambitious classmates in Beida in 1977 fresh from taking the reinstituted *gaokao*, the young protesters in Tiananmen Square in 1989, and the rock throwers in front of the U.S. Embassy in 1999 protesting the accidental bombing of the Chinese Embassy in Belgrade during the Balkan wars.

Youth is kinetic energy. They are carefree, irreverent, and rebellious. They are the first to embrace new ideas and trends, but when things go wrong, they are also the first to rush to the barricades, burn tires and even throw Molotov cocktails, to demand change. I was that way. I sang American protest songs. I protested in the streets. I joined a trip to discover how Mao and communism were changing China. That's how I got here.

But what direction will this latest generation of Chinese students take?

The Chinese under the age of twenty-four are a staggering demographic. They now number about 700 million, like their own nation. They are driving changes in China with their sheer numbers. Their likes and dislikes and their life decisions condition the policies and actions of China's leadership.

This generation does not remember the Cultural Revolution or feel its legacy. Their parents had to depend on the work unit they were assigned to — that guaranteed cradle-to-grave jobs, food and shelter. Citizens had a child-like dependence on the government. No longer. Responsibility for housing, education, health care, employment and retirement has now been rudely shoved onto the shoulders of this millennial generation. Young people must now acquire survival skills that their parents never learned.

To pursue their driving ambitions, many young people are adapting to the new swim-or-sink world. Nearly 50% of China's millennials — those born after 1995 — are breaking away from the traditional job market, according to a survey conducted in 2016 by QQ Browser, part of Tencent Holdings Ltd. The study, which polled 13,000 college students and mined data from its 84-million daily online searchers, found significant hints on the likes, dislikes and aspirations of China's post-reform youth.

What jobs are they seeking? Over 15% of the respondents aspire to start their own businesses; 8% want to break into professions spawned by consumerism and the growing role of the Internet. The most sought-after jobs? Online live-streamer or blogger, voice actor, make-up artist and game tester.

Everything is so new there are few role models to follow. Their parents taught them to study hard and make as much money as quickly as they could. Religion is a distant concept to most young Chinese, and they have found little with which to replace it. It is very easy to despair at the all-embracing materialism that they see everywhere around them. No wonder the recurring themes in contemporary Chinese art and literature focus on alienation and cynicism.

The ferocious rat race has warped youth culture and work ethic. Recently young people have embraced a grueling "996" culture—working from 9am to 9pm, six days a week—that was popularized by China's uber-billionaire entrepreneurs like Alibaba founder Jack Ma. Now, they are pushing back against the culture that equates money and success with happiness. They advocate *tang ping* (lying flat), an online buzzword that mirrors their changing priorities and disillusionment with the oppressive work culture. Instead of keeping up with rising expectations of the society and corporate China, many are choosing to simply *tang ping*, scraping by with minimum effort. "It's a mindset that individual efforts cannot reverse the organization and societal change," explains Alex Shi, a twenty-something who works for a multinational company in Beijing. "To acknowledge this, you just do the bare minimum to get by."

Two young women I know represent different ways of dealing with this generational crisis.

Jia Ruimin, who I mentioned earlier in this chapter, typifies the new Beida spirit: her ambitions are laser-focused and yet she is versatile. She studies hard, shops with friends, participates in the Sino-Japanese Exchange Society, the Volleyball Club as well as being president of the Traditional Chinese Music Club. She watches soap operas too.

Her father is a policeman in Shanxi province and her mother is an employee in a food company there. For Jia, passing the *gaokao* and getting into Beida opened several prospective career choices. When she graduates from medical school in 2022, she will also have an undergraduate degree with a double major in Biomedical English and Economics. She hopes to take a master's program in health and humanities at a London university and is feverishly leveling up her language skills. She already gets very high scores in mock TOEFL exams but is not complacent. She told me she aims to become a simultaneous interpreter specializing in health care—a newly minted career.

It used to be that even graduates of elite schools like Beida had limited opportunities. They got plum offers but if they chose not to take the job, they'd remain unemployed. However, once in the job, they would discover it difficult or impossible to transfer elsewhere.

Today, Beida students have many career opportunities. They may find jobs in the private sector, start a business or apply to study overseas. And that's part of the stress: too many choices, too many uncertainties, too many applications and tests and requirements and hoops to jump through. And the future is unclear. Jobs available now may not be there forever. Jia Ruimin aspires to do graduate school in London and stay in the UK or Europe for a few years, but she has qualms. "I'm a little worried about finding internships and jobs in the future," she says. "I guess the job market is not too promising anywhere in the world."

Li Yuansi was still a senior in one of Beijing's top high schools when I met her. She had chosen an English name for herself: Alice. She was attending a Beida forum for likely enrollees where I was a speaker. Not quite eighteen, she wanted to get into a good college but detested the prospect of grueling *gaokao* examinations.

She had asked four fellow senior high students in her class if they thought *gaokao* was worth the trouble. They all agreed it was better than the old system because there is little chance of cheating or "backdoorism" — a practice of giving special pass to children of officials and rich families. Still, they said, some *gaokao* policies are not fair, such as giving bonus points for ethnic minority students. They also agreed that a single test cannot comprehensively — and fairly — evaluate a college applicant.

Several weeks before graduation, Yuansi's four classmates took the *gaokao* and passed. Yuansi did not even take it. In 2016, she left for Seattle to pursue college education. In 2020, she earned her degree in Industrial Design from the University of Washington in Seattle and soon landed a job in Meredith Corporation, an American media company. She has acculturated well in America she even joins open mic sessions at comedy bars but remains connected with her Chinese roots. She has stopped using "Alice". "It was a nickname I got in elementary school, and it didn't mean anything to me," she explains. "Yuansi is my legal name and I love the beautiful meaning behind it. It means 'the first idea'."

The world beyond China has always been a way to relieve pressure. But globalization may have peaked and journeys to the West are no longer assured. What happens now? And is there anything Xi Jinping and the Communist Party can do?

People in Beijing like to joke about how times have changed. In the 1970s, Chinese people typically asked *ni chifan le meiyou?* (Have you eaten yet?) whenever they met friends on the street — reflecting the scarcity of the times. In the 1980s, they tended to ask *ni chuguo le meiyou?* (Have you traveled overseas yet?), reflecting the openness that China was allowing itself. In the

1990s, that greeting changed to *ni li le meiyou?* (Are you divorced yet?), reflecting the changing social mores. And today? People rarely greet each other because they are all looking down at their phones, scrolling through social media, watching a TV drama, or playing online games.

One thing hasn't changed: the primacy of the Communist Party. If one believes in it — and behaves accordingly — one can do almost anything one wants. In a high-level forum for ideological and political teachers in 2019, Xi Jinping — who is the country's most powerful person as Communist Party chief — highlighted the "guiding position of Marxism" when teaching politics and ideology in schools. Xi asked teachers to "nurture generation after generation of young people who support Communist Party rule and China's socialist system."

All of this old terminology obscures one thing: No one really knows what the Communist Party is ultimately about. With its ninety million members, it remains the most efficient political organization in the country, and possibly the world. Indeed, it is guaranteed by the constitution to be the only party allowed in power. But the Maoist vision of a Marxist, egalitarian paradise is viewed by many Chinese as irrelevant in their daily lives, which is all about making money, encouraged by Deng's admonition "allow some people to get rich first." At least that was the case for forty years. And then came the "common prosperity" policy in 2021, which aims at making Chinese society more egalitarian by spreading prosperity at a modest level amongst wider swathes of society.

The new mantra requires yet another radical shift in Chinese mindset. For decades since the communist takeover of China, the Communist Party had pushed a series of socialist political campaigns driven by class warfare. In the 1960s, for instance, they set off mass mobilization attacking the "Four Olds" —

Old Customs. Old Culture, Old Habits and Old Ideas. During the tumultuous Cultural Revolution (1966-76), they attacked "capitalist-roaders" and reactionaries. They condemned such traditional philosophies—Buddhism, Taoism, Confucianism, along with Christianity and other religions. In their place, the Party imposed Maoist orthodoxy, "Fight selfishness!", the masses were admonished. "Serve the people!" After the death of Chairman Mao in 1976 and the ascension of Deng Xiaoping, however, a series of campaigns eroded Maoist orthodoxy, leaving the masses confused and cynical. The noble goal of working for the common good was largely discredited and discarded. *Yiqie xiang qian kan* (put money above everything else) became the new mantra. That's a clever pun that sounds like "go forward-looking for everything."

For more people in China now, money-making remains the over-riding goal—even though most people are aware of the hollowness of that quest. The media bemoans "money-worship" and there has been much in recent decades of China facing a *xinyang weiji* (crisis of belief), or a *jingshen kongxu* (spiritual void) with concomitant egotism, social malaise and lawlessness. Aware that they are spiritually adrift, many Chinese are searching for a moral compass, a mooring. Some find them in religion; others turn to cults.

The Communist Party has been scrambling to find alternatives to fill the void, and one answer is the "rejuvenation of China," even though for some, the jingoistic shibboleth echoes old Maoist revolutionary spirit that creates a sense of unease. Other people advocate the revival of traditional culture and a novel amalgamation of the Buddhist, Taoist and Confucian philosophies that hark back to the faded glories of the Middle Kingdom. Perhaps the solution, they say, is a non-socialist Confucian hybrid that attempts to link the 2,500-year-old way of thinking to economic growth and prosperity, as typified by the experiences of Taiwan, South Korea and Singapore.

There is a more dangerous prescription: nationalism. It appeals to the Chinese historical imagination, which laments that the Middle Kingdom—once so advanced and prosperous compared to the rest of the world—was bullied and humiliated by Western powers and Japan. These rising powers exploited China's weaknesses to wrest territory and privileges from an empire in decline. The memory of such humiliating treatment can be painful and inflammatory for Chinese people.

I am baffled by the over-riding importance that the Chinese give to "face" — a sense of pride that they value disproportionately. Any act, comment, tone of voice or even facial expression that hints at criticism or rejection, especially if it happens in front of other people, could lead to "loss of face", *diu mianzi* in Chinese. The century-long loss of face to foreign powers still causes ruptures, and the government does not allow it to fade into history because it helps to provide legitimacy.

The Chinese can pledge to open up, they can covet things foreign, and yet, in many ways, these responses are a cover for a deep insecurity. There is a paradoxical two-facedness, what they call *nei wai you bie*—*this* for outside consumption, and *that* for internal use only. It is a sensitivity that I and other veterans of China-watching tiptoe around. And few acts can cause a reaction as strong and irrational as denying that China should expect redress from its historic defeats.

Hence, the nationalist push and popular support for a strong state, including acceptance of its more intrusive surveillance powers. China has to be strong in order to face down its foreign enemies, and that means everyone at home must behave and toe the line. Religious leaders cannot contravene faith in the Communist Party and the state that it steers. Everyone must be willing to make sacrifices to avoid disruptions that could bring China back to its weak old days. The citizenry is reminded of its ability to *chiku* (eat bitterness) — the high threshold for putting up with pain, inconvenience and maltreatment that is part of the myth of contemporary China. How else could they have survived civil war, Cultural Revolution, mass starvation and the totalitarian whims of Mao? The Chinese are reminded again and again by state-sponsored popular culture that they can *chiku* better than anyone else.

Another commonality is an aversion to *luan* (chaos) — the very situation that makes *chiku* a necessity in the first place. For millennia, Chinese rulers have had to grapple with the ideas of luan and zhi (control). China's ancient philosopher Confucius, who lived in a chaotic time, preached the need for social and political authority and hierarchy to achieve social harmony. He believed that a society without hierarchy would lapse into chaos. Mencius, a prominent follower of Confucius, came up with the notion of the Mandate of Heaven, by which the emperor, or Son of Heaven, is given semidivine authority to rule, Linda Jaivin explains in her book The Shortest History of China. "Mencius described politics as a cycle of 'order and chaos'," Jaivin writes. "If an emperor forsook his mandate through immoral behavior or incompetence, rebellion and dynastic change was justified."

Constant fear of losing the Mandate of Heaven prompts rulers to err on the side of order, including the suppression of dissent. In so far as a great number of Chinese people share their rulers' fear of chaos, they assent to such controls in order to assure harmony. So far, this compulsive fixation on preserving social harmony while struggling for personal and national advancement has made the new China resourceful, resilient, patient and strong. But for how much longer? It is a troubling center of gravity for a modern national identity.

I am awed by how China has changed over the past five decades, as it moved from a poor, isolated country to become a dominant world power. In 1985, when China was just revving up Deng Xiaoping's reform, my TIME Magazine colleague Richard Hornik and I interviewed several scholars, economists and political leaders for a cover story on what we would call China's Second Revolution. Actor-playwright Ying Ruocheng gave us the best quote in describing the Dengist reform. In flawless English, Ying said: "We are trying to compress the Renaissance, the Reformation and the Industrial Revolution into a single decade." It's been more than a decade but the transformation, in my lifetime, has been nothing short of a miracle.

And so, despite demographics and pandemics, I tend to remain optimistic that China will, sooner or later, overcome its problems. Whenever China seemed to reverse course from its progressive trajectory of reform and opening up, I'd say "it's just a tactical retreat, part of the ebb and flow of China's reform that I have seen all these years." One step back, two steps forward.

Of course, I need to temper my optimism. China is changing, sometimes dramatically, sometimes glacially, but always unevenly. China's leaders, who were in their teens and early twenties during the Cultural Revolution, are primarily concerned with avoiding a return to chaos. When faced with the choice of pushing reform — even modest political reform — and avoiding chaos, they typically choose the status quo. *Qiuwen* — go steady — that is their instinctive preference.

I see jarring juxtapositions wherever I turn: migrant workers grunting through the city streets using sheer brawn to haul loads of bricks and steel pipes; Ferraris zoom past fancy new skyscraper just a few blocks away from virtual slums where migrants share decrepit communal toilets.

China has been pursuing change in the half-start, pragmatic way for more than a century—even before the founding of Beida—"feeling the stones while crossing the river," as Chinese officials in the Deng era put it. Across China, the old ways mix and clash with the new. It is an uneasy coexistence. So much more needs to happen. And hundreds of millions of people are waiting impatiently, even desperately, for the future.

Chairman Mao's remains are still kept in a glass sarcophagus inside a mausoleum in Tiananmen Square. Every day, thousands of people line up to pay respects to the late Great Leader, who is on display like the undecayed corpse of some Buddhist or Catholic saint.

Just south of the Square, not far from Mao's mausoleum, is a Kentucky Fried Chicken restaurant. In the early 1980s, I covered the opening ceremony of the fast-food chain's first branch in China's capital. A life-size porcelain bust of founder Colonel Sanders was displayed at the entrance—similar but different from the worshipful statuary of the Chairman himself. Mao must be wincing, I thought. Thirty or so years later, the American fast-food outlet is still doing brisk business selling finger-lickin' chicken to hordes of Chinese. And now, there are innumerable home-grown fast-food chains in the People's Republic itself.

The Chairman and the Colonel. I've managed to see them both ensconced at the center of Chinese power. And the revolutions keep happening. I have witnessed a sea change since I arrived in the 1970s. I saw the reign of the Red Guard. I saw China as drab as a Mao suit, a country poor and isolated and hostile to the wider world. I witnessed the People's Republic fractured by Chairman Mao's injunction that, to remain faithful to Communist tenets, the Party must pursue "class struggle". For years, families, communities, work units and most of the society were splintered according to classes – one either belongs to a revolutionary or a counter-revolutionary class. One huge billboard in Beijing's main intersections was emblazoned with the Chairman's ubiquitous slogan: "Never Forget Class Struggle."

Then with Deng's market-opening reforms, the ideological billboards gave way to advertisements for Nokia phones and Remy Martin XO. Over the years, China became more and more tightly linked with the global community, through business and trade, diplomacy, tourism, sports, educational exchanges and the Internet. China became porous to outside influences, from Hollywood to the NBA, Starbucks and Ikea.

That is now changing again. In the past few years, under Xi Jinping, public political slogans have made a solid comeback. It is not yet clear how far he will go toward the Maoist past.

China is no longer the "poor man of Asia." The shift away from Maoist economic policies has turned it into the second biggest economy in the world. Thanks to a sustained economic boom, China has morphed from a socialist dystopia into a vibrant "state capitalist" economy. And it is not just an economic power. The People's Liberation Army is no longer a "junkyard army" wearing baggy pants and canvas shoes and carrying AK-47s. It has emerged as a formidable and rapidly modernizing military power, boasting of a blue-water navy, capable of launching humans into space and shooting down satellites. Washington politicians and pundits cannot stop talking about the threat of China to American dominance.

But China's prosperity has come at a heavy price. Its economic leap forward in the past four decades has been accompanied by a slew of unintended consequences: regionalism, corruption, a widening income gap, ecological degradation a mountain of debt, spiritual void and social instability. The country is confronting a long-term demographic challenge as a result of its "one couple, one-child," policy. Adopted in the late 1970s, it slowed down population growth and fostered prosperity. But in a nation of small families, millions of single-child couples now have to look after two sets of elderly parents, causing a strain on the family's resources and the government's social welfare network. Despite its enormous youth cohort, China's population is aging very rapidly. All these challenges are pulling the country in a thousand directions.

If China is so littered with sociological tinder, will it implode? I think that's unlikely.

Chinese people are generally resourceful, resilient and patient. As I've observed earlier in this book, they can *chiku* (eat bitterness). It is considered a virtue. For the older generation, the dark days of the Cultural Revolution are still living memory. There is a shared aversion to *"luan"* (chaos).

All that has benefitted the Communist Party — which promises peace in exchange for control. It has used the media, education and artificial intelligence effectively to manage public opinion and popular expectations. The army and the police are arms of the party, not the state.

I see a complex China in a state of flux. As a journalist who has seen the country's explosive development over four decades, I have marveled at the economic and technological revolutions that have transformed the whole country. At the same time, I am deeply saddened by the wanton destruction of Beijing's cultural heritage — the demolition of *siheyuan* (courtyard houses), some centuries-old, to make way for soulless shopping malls, elevated bridges, ring roads and subway lines. I despair over the destruction of the social fabric of old neighborhoods formed on the basis of the *hutong* as developers build luxury condos and gated communities. Others share my feelings.

The Peace Hotel, where I stayed early in my life in Beijing, is now unrecognizable from the simple building where I survived the great earthquake of 1976. Today, high-rise buildings dwarf the once humble neighborhood. On one corner, the courtyards have been torn down and replaced by showrooms for Porsche and Maserati.

The Xiangjiang State Farm, where I labored for several months in the early 1970s, planting rice, feeding pigs and digging ditches — is now gone. The local government has relocated workers and their families and auctioned off the farmland to real estate developers. The last time I revisited Xiangjiang in 2016, all I could see was a highway and rows of commercial housing. I could not find a single worker I knew.

China is a cocktail of contradictions. It remains hidebound in ancient tradition and conventions, and yet it is quick to embrace new concepts and practices. It's one of the oldest civilizations, and yet it is still trying to catch up with others as a modern, developed country.

China has changed in huge numbers of ways but the system — the relationships between the Communist Party, the state and the people of China and the world — fundamentally remains the same as when I arrived. Xi Jinping, the Communist Party chief and state president since 2012, has consolidated power. He holds all the No. 1 positions and is also described as China's COE — chief of everything. In 2018, he maneuvered to revise the Communist Party constitution, removing term limits on his top post, thus allowing him to stay in power beyond his second five-year term in 2023.

Soon after Xi took up his paramount posts in 2012, he called on the youth to "dare to dream, work to fulfill your dreams and contribute to the rejuvenation of the nation." This is now known as *Zhongguo Meng*, or China Dream, which he described as improvement of people's livelihood, prosperity, military strengthening and national rejuvenation. Not to be confused with the American Dream, it's about seeking individual and collective prosperity and realization of socialism. It is also about recapturing China's standing in the global stage, a triumphant comeback of the Middle Kingdom.

Xi is clearly thinking of what legacy he will leave behind. He envisions China in 2049, the 100th year founding anniversary of the People's Republic. By that time, Xi envisions China as an advanced country with a modern economy and society on par with the United States. If China achieves that goal, Xi could claim that as a validation of the Communist Party's "great, glorious, and correct" leadership—and of his own legacy. How China uses its new and growing wealth and power in the regional and global order remains an open question.

I expect Xi Jinping and the new generation of leaders to pursue China's modernization goals with the same drive and fervor as their predecessors. Most of them are technocrats—pragmatic and results-driven. They will seek sustained economic growth and social stability. They will push to propel China as a global superpower and they will make Chinese proud. Their claim to the "mandate of heaven" — to right to continue its rule over China— largely rests on those three goals. But their ultimate objective will be to ensure the Communist Party's uninterrupted rule over the country. If any of these efforts to reform and modernize start to jeopardize that over-riding goal, they will be delayed or scuttled altogether.

Meantime, there is one other thing that remains constant in China: the importance that the Chinese put on education. In the same way that the storied Class of 1977 pursued learning to change their lives, and to change China, the young generation today are doing the same: seeking knowledge.

***

Several meters up a small hill, next to Weiming Lake, is a place I go for serenity in Beida. There is a bench in this corner of the lakeshore and, in between my class lectures, I sit here and read or listen to music on my old iPod.

A few steps away is the site of the tomb of Edgar Snow, the American journalist and writer championed by the Party as "a friend of the Chinese people", even as his detractors say he had wittingly served as a propaganda tool of Chairman Mao's communist regime. Snow worked as a journalist in Shanghai in the 1930s and taught part-time at Beida. He interviewed Mao Zedong in the caves of Yan'an, then the headquarters of the communist survivors of the Long March. With his 1937 book *Red Star Over China*, a seminal portrait of Mao and his ragtag communist army, Snow became one of the first Western reporters to introduce Mao and the Chinese communist movement to readers in the West, even though there are people who view him as having been a propaganda tool, witting or unwitting, of the Party.

In December 1970, during his last visit to China, Snow was invited to stand next to Mao on the rostrum of the Gate of Heavenly Peace, overlooking the square that takes its name from the old portal—Tiananmen, or Gate of Heavenly Peace. There, they watched a celebration of the anniversary of the founding of the People's Republic. The Chairman then asked the journalist to join him for an informal talk, which turned out to last five hours. He told Snow that he was willing to welcome Richard Nixon on a visit to Beijing in whatever capacity the American president wished. That olive-branch interview—Snow's final one with Mao—was published by TIME Magazine soon after. On July 15 of the following year, Nixon announced he would travel to China. Snow, however, would not live to see the historic state visit, dying of pancreatic cancer the week Nixon flew to Beijing in February 1972. At that point, I was learning about life in rural China, working as a farmer in Hunan, Mao's hometown. I'd been in the People's Republic for almost a year.

Snow's remains are not entirely by Weiming Lake. As he directed in his will, half of his ashes are in the Hudson River town of Sneden's Landing, a half-hour drive north of New York City. It was a fitting division. He was a man who shared his life with two countries. In a small way, I see much of myself reflected in Snow. He was an American who found himself in a troubled China and did what he thought was best to bring it forward to join the rest of the world. I am a Filipino who found myself in a troubled China and have lived to see it prosper in the world even as it struggles to find its modern soul. It's been a long road since I journeyed to China and joined the Class of '77. History has its portents, and the future is yet beckoning bright.

ACKNOWLEDGMENTS

My story is enriched by the wonderful characters who came into my life. I am immensely grateful to:

My siblings Nieva, Irma, Rene, Nilo and Leni for standing by me in good times and even in times when I seemed like the "black sheep" brother

Chito Sta. Romana, Eric Baculinao, Rey Tiquia, and Grace Punongbayan, my fellow Filipino exiles in China

Zhang Jinwei, Wenran Jiang, and Li Xiaocong, my Peking University roommates

Howard Chua-Eoan, my former editor at TIME Magazine, for shepherding me all the way in writing this book

Graham Earnshaw, publisher of this book, for liking my story and putting up with my procrastination to finally get it done

Jan Wong, for prompting me to apply for a parttime researcher's job that led to more

Melinda Liu and Richard Bernstein for giving me my Beijing reporter's jobs

Gay Talese and Nan Talese, John Papanek and Jackie Judd, Eleanor and Prod Laquian for motivating me to write a memoir

Richard Hornik, Jay Branegan, Linda Jaivin, Don Morrison, Ed Gargan, Peter Wolff, Frank Hawke, Tim Stanley, Mike Revzin, Cristina Dc Pastor and many other friends for sending comments and corrections on my manuscript

Tang Shan, my departed benefactor in Changsha, Hunan Province

Liu Anyi and his wife Li Dilan, for opening their cramped flat — and kitchen — to me, a stateless Filipino and a frequent visitor in the late 1970s, when it was still not "correct" to receive foreigners at home

Frank and Ruth Coe, Sol Adler and Rose Smith, long-time expats in Beijing, for lending me English-language books from their extensive home libraries

Huang Lanyou, for allowing me to stay for several months in his spare room while I waited for housing allocation

Hou Dejian, Taiwanese singer-composer who defected to the mainland in 1983, with whom I shared a flat, songs and many adventures in the '80s, and Geremie Barmé, who introduced me to Hou, and shared with me many insights on China

Song Mingjiang, Liu Lianli and Lü Binghong, my Mandarin teachers

Wang Xiaoqiu, Zhou Nanjing, Ke Gao, Huang Daolin, Cai Huosheng, Wang Wenquan, my Peking University mentors

Chen Yanni, Bai Weiji, Hu Ping, Wang Juntao, Fengming Liu, Yang Baikui, Zha Jianying, Zhou Yuan, Wang Yan, Mu Zining, Hao Ping, Zhang Baijia, Li Bo, Zhang Feifei, Ying Da, and other members of Class '77, Class '78 and Class '79 and Class '78 for sharing stories and insights for this book

Tang Wenfang, Fang Yang, Sun Zhi, Xu Lei, Shen Wenyu, Zhu Lijing, Yang Qingxian, Li Qi, Wang Shizhou, Ou Weijia, Yuan Gang, Xu Kangjiang, fellow members of the Peking University men's varsity team

Kongkeo Mongkongvilay, Shanthi Wikkramasinha, Peter Hegetschweiler, David Hsieh, Ted Lipman, Dickson Hall, David Zweig, Ivan Kinsella, Asai Chie, Anniki Arponen, Lars Peter Freden, Lena Sun, Stan Herschorn, Donald Clarke, Uwe

Richter, Ming-bao Yue, Ming-chu Yue, Stefan Simons, Tim Gellatt, James Feinerman, Lia Guthers, Lisa Hsia, Christophe Jung, Akira Yagi, Asta Kristjansdottir, Tryggvi Hardarson, Hjöleifu Sveinbjörnsson, Patty Wen, Greg Lee, Mulatu Teshome, Paola Paderni, Ragnar Baldursson, Johnny Erling and many other fellow Peking University enrollees in the '70s

Nancy Sta. Romana, Peng Wenlan, Huang Wei, Nancy Berliner, Boriana Song, Li Yan, Romy Garcia, Marisse Garcia, Huang Yong, Bao Yin, Victor Li Weijia, Ding Lili, Todd Carrel, Julia Chen, Carl Walter, Andrew Andreasen, Carl Crook, Marni Rosner, Roberta Lipson, Ted Plafker, Elyse Silverman, Jim Spear, Tang Liang, Victor Ochoa, Jim Laurie, Barbara Alighiero, Meg Maggio, Liu Heung Shing, Jim McGregor, John Holden, Alan Babington Smith, Jen Lin-Liu, Hong Huang, Idriz Celmeta, Francesco Sisci, Kaiser Kuo, Andy Friend, Jin Xing, Li Chun, Mike Boccio, Sophia Wong, Rey Lao Lim, Guada Sanchez McLauchlan, Jun Gonzales, Vlad Reyes, Teresa Reyes, Elmer Reyes, Dory Poa, Asuncion Benitez, Ed Cua, Michael Tan, Mercy Dujunco, Hope Ngo, Sally Young, Jim and Susie Brown, Bill Valentino, Serge Dumont, Nancy Roth Remington, Jiang Xueqin, Erna Marcus, Joseph Loftus, Rebecca Xu and Benjamin Kang Lim, good friends from various sectors who shared my keen interests in news and in things Chinese

Peter Hessler, Frank Langfitt, John Pomfret, Mark Leong, Scott Kronick, Jim Gradoville, Matt Forney, Peter Schuer, Mike Myer, Jim Moriarty, Bob Saget, Ma Jian, Kai Yang, Craig Simons, Paul Mooney, Scott Savitt and Peter Wonacott, for sharing my passion for basketball in our Sunday pickup games

Henry Grunwald, John Stacks, Sandra Burton, Henry Muller, Karsten Prager, Jim Kelly, Richard Duncan, Joelle Attinger,

Adi Ignatius, Pico Iyer, Ed Reingold, Barry Hillenbrand, Robin Moyer and Mia Turner, for showing me elegant writing and dogged journalism

Ted Turner, Eason Jordan, Parisa Khosravi, Richard Griffiths, Richard Roth, Ellana Lee, Mei Yan, Wen-Chun Fan, Jeff King, Brad Olson, Lisa Rose Weaver, Tara Duffy, Susie Xu, Mike Chinoy, Andrea Koppel, Rebecca McKinnon, John Vause, Emily Chang and Stan Grant for training me in how to tell stories in two minutes or less

Steven Jiang, Chen Xiaoni, Yuli Yang, Hong Haolan, Shao Tian, CY Xu, Zhang Dayu, Judy Kwon and Sherisse Pham, my former CNN Beijing bureau colleagues, for helping in research

Nona Zaldivar, for helping me secure a new Philippine passport, and her sister Lorna and brother-in-law Raul Segovia, for embracing me into the Zaldivar-Segovia clan

Ofelia Buluran and Peace Corps Volunteer Douglas Nossaman, my high school English teachers and school paper advisers

Nemesio Prudente, the late president of Philippine College of Commerce, who turned our "poor man's college" into a hotbed of political activism and a top-notch university

Vicente Wenceslao, Angie Castillo, Al Mendoza, Sol Juvida, Edd Aragon, and Etel Dionisio, who fearlessly co-published our college newspaper *Ang Malaya* (The Free)

Jo-Ann Maglipon, Elso Cabangon, Antonio Tagamolila, Leopoldo "Babes" Calixto, Jessica Sales, Jack Peña, Evelyn Pacheco, Leticia Pascual, Manuel Bautista, Fred Bat-og and Roberto Coloma, members of the College Editors Guild of the Philippines (1969-72) who fought the Marcos dictatorship with their pens — and paid a hefty price

About The Author

Jaime FlorCruz is a veteran China-watcher and one of the longest-serving foreign correspondents in China. While on a three-week study tour of China in 1971, FlorCruz was forced into political exile from his Philippine homeland and unexpectedly found himself stranded in China at the height of the tumultuous Cultural Revolution. He worked on a state farm in Hunan province, Mao Zedong's birthplace, and also in a state fishing company in Shandong Province, and then studied the Chinese language and history at university in Beijing. Following China's opening in the late 1970s, he got work as a journalist with Newsweek and later spent many years working as a correspondent for TIME Magazine and CNN out of Beijing. FlorCruz has witnessed and reported on the most significant events in China's past four decades and more, including the country's economic and social reform. He still lives in Beijing and is an adjunct professor at Peking University.